Your First Marine Aquarium

John H. Tullock

Your First Marine Aquarium

Everything About Setting Up a Marine
Aquarium, Including Conditioning,
Maintenance, Selecting Fish and
Invertebrates, and More

Filled with Full-color Photographs

BARRON'S

CONTENTS

INTRODUCTION

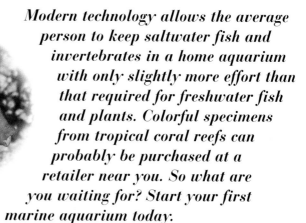

Modern technology allows the average person to keep saltwater fish and invertebrates in a home aquarium with only slightly more effort than that required for freshwater fish and plants. Colorful specimens from tropical coral reefs can probably be purchased at a retailer near you. So what are you waiting for? Start your first marine aquarium today.

When I was a kid, my mom and dad took me to the beach in South Carolina. I brought home three surf clams and kept them alive for a while in a jar with some sand and ocean water. This began for me a lifelong interest in the fascinating creatures of the sea. After graduate school, I taught a course called "Coral Reef Ecology." I also worked with ichthyologist Dr. Dave Etnier. These experiences helped to focus my interest on the uniqueness and beauty of coral reef ecosystems. The undersea equivalent of a tropical rain forest, coral reefs provide a living demonstration of myriad principles of modern ecology. For every adaptive strategy ecologists can categorize, on the reef there probably exists a "textbook" example of a species using that strategy. Exhibiting coral reef organisms in

Coral reefs shelter an astonishing diversity of life, often remarkably colorful, such as this harlequin tuskfish (Choerodon fasciatus).

aquaria is undoubtedly one of the best ways for human beings to become familiar with a shining example of nature's exuberance.

I have designed marine aquariums for purposes of research and exhibition of coral reef organisms since 1980. Since then, changes in our knowledge have made the old designs obsolete. Successful long-term aquarium systems—even exhibiting some of the reef's most delicate organisms—can easily be designed and maintained by a hobbyist. It is fair to say that the finest examples of captive reef ecosystems have been created by private individuals enjoying their leisure time, the considerable accomplishments of public aquariums notwithstanding.

However, I suggest you give some serious thought to the undertaking before you decide to become involved in the marine aquarium hobby. A marine aquarium requires a commitment of time and can cost a significant amount of money. However, both time and

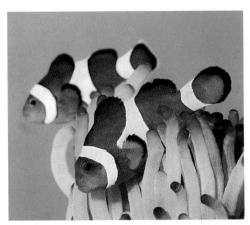

A pair of clownfish (**Amphiprion ocellaris**) *cavort in a marine aquarium.*

strategies, let me just say that the wealth of information available on any conceivable topic leaves little excuse for ignorance. Among the more useful Web sites is FishBase, a comprehensive database of information on thousands of fish, both marine and freshwater. The URL is *www.fishbase.org/search.php.*

As you read, make notes. Create a list of fish and/or invertebrate species that you think you might like to have in your proposed aquarium. Write down any questions that arise, and then get the answers. This may be from further reading, counsel from an experienced friend, or from a Web site. Most importantly, decide how much space, time, and money you can reasonably devote to the project. Having a plan will spare you frustration, not to mention expense.

Over the years, I have developed what I like to call my "Five Rules for a Successful Aquarium."

1. Keep it simple.

Pay more attention to maintaining good water quality, providing proper nutrition, and carrying out regular maintenance, and less attention to installing the latest piece of high-tech equipment. Fancy equipment cannot substitute for proper husbandry. Start with a basic system and learn to maintain it properly. Then you will be better able to decide wisely if additional equipment will really help you to get more enjoyment out of the hobby. Some aquarium dealers are interested only in selling you more equipment, and their sales pitches are sometimes hard for the beginner to judge. If you think you are being pressured, you probably are correct. Find another dealer; there are plenty of good ones out there who deserve your business.

2. Keep it roomy.

Marine fish require ample space. How much space depends not only upon the mature size of

money are well-rewarded by the entertainment and educational value of a thriving miniature ecosystem aquarium. One can achieve a deep sense of accomplishment from watching the developments in a properly designed aquarium. Arriving at a good design requires some effort. You must learn about the biology of the organisms you plan to keep, and then use this information to plan the aquarium carefully. Your reward comes when you get to sit in your family room and watch some of the ocean's denizens behaving as if they were swimming on an authentic coral reef. Because reef organisms come in such variety and reef habitats are so complex, there is no substitute for knowledge when it comes to marine aquarium keeping. Books are the best source of all the basic information in one convenient place. Therefore, read as much as possible.

Utilize the many online resources available. Typing "marine aquarium" into a search engine will yield hundreds of thousands of hits. Rather than digress into a discussion of Internet search the fish, but also upon the nature of its lifestyle. Fish that normally remain within a comparatively small territory, such as clownfish, tend to accept confinement in an aquarium more readily than wide-ranging species such as tangs. Even the largest aquarium is tiny when compared to the vast ocean around a coral reef. Most likely, the size of the tank you choose will be determined by the availability of space and money. If you only have room or money for a 10-gallon (38 L) tank, it is foolish to select a fish that requires a 50-gallon (189 L) tank. Choose species that are in proportion to the size of the miniature ecosystem you are designing. Resist the temptation to add "just one more fish," when common sense (not to mention the reference books) says the tank is at capacity.

3. Keep it stable.

The coral reef, the source of the fish and invertebrate species offered for sale in the aquarium trade, is among the most stable environments on earth. Temperature, salinity, dissolved oxygen, water clarity, even the length of the day, are confined to narrow ranges in comparison to freshwater and terrestrial habitats, or even temperate oceanic habitats. Corals themselves, the basis for the existence of the reef ecosystem, only occur where water conditions are appropriate. This is why reefs are only found in certain geographical areas. Reef fish and invertebrates have therefore not evolved adaptive strategies to cope with rapid fluctuations in environmental conditions. This is in marked contrast to freshwater fish, which come from waters that experience drastic changes throughout the course of the seasons. Maintaining stability in a marine tank requires reliable equipment. You must perform required maintenance consistently. You must regularly

The yellow tang (**Zebrasoma flavescens**) *ranks as one of the best of its family for beginning aquarists.*

carry out water analysis and adjust conditions appropriately. I call this aspect of marine aquarium keeping "test and tweak." You assess conditions by testing, then tweak them back in line if they lie outside the optimal range.

4. Keep it clean.

Aside from the issues of appearance and basic hygiene, keeping the aquarium "clean" or, more precisely, "nutrient poor," is the single best way to avoid an excessive growth of algae. Excessive algae growth usually occurs when too much phosphate accumulates in the aquarium water. This happens because the aquarium lacks the

Large, aggressive fish, like the clown trigger (Balistoides conspicillum) will need a roomy tank and robust tank mates.

dynamic nutrient cycling process that occurs on natural reefs. There are some standard rules, of course: feed sparingly; remove dead organic matter promptly; siphon out debris regularly; and carry out water changes as necessary. To control algae, do not allow phosphate to accumulate. For example, phosphate is released when food is metabolized by any organism. Phosphates can enter the tank from external sources, also. Some salt mixes contain phosphate. Tap water supplies can also contain this nutrient.

5. Keep it natural.

Try to duplicate to the fullest extent possible the conditions under which your marine specimens were living while in the ocean. Thoroughly investigate the ecology of any species in which you are interested before you purchase a specimen. While the majority of fish offered for sale in aquarium shops require essentially the same water conditions (remember what was said earlier about the narrow range of vari-

ation in the reef environment), they may differ quite significantly in size and temperament. Some are quite tolerant, others extremely finicky. Successful aquarium husbandry often depends upon understanding such differences between species. Scientific knowledge about the ecology of any species always provides the most satisfactory guide to supplying its needs in a captive environment.

Another aspect of aquarium "cleanliness" has to do with the tolerance by marine fish of poisonous waste products, such as ammonia, which can accumulate in the closed system of the aquarium if the aquarist does not create the appropriate biological system to permit detoxification and recycling. One of the major physiological differences between marine fish and their freshwater counterparts is their relationship to the watery medium. In freshwater fish, the body fluids are saltier than the water surrounding them, so they constantly absorb water

Delicate species, like the mandarin dragonet (**Synchiropus splendidus**) *should be given their own tanks.*

by osmosis, creating the danger of fluid over-load. To compensate for this, freshwater fish rarely drink water, and their kidneys excrete copious urine to rid their bodies of excess water. In marine fish, the body fluids are more dilute than the surrounding sea. Thus, they lose water to their surroundings, and ironically are in constant danger of dehydration. To compen-sate, marine fish drink seawater, and excrete relatively small amounts of concentrated urine. In either marine or freshwater fish, only water itself enters or leaves the tissues via osmosis. Substances in the water generally must enter the body via ingestion. Since they ingest water continually, marine fish are therefore much more susceptible to poisoning from pollutants than are freshwater fish. All fish excrete ammo-nia into the water, but marine fish are far less tolerant of any accumulation of this waste product than are freshwater fish. This means not only that there must be adequate waste

detoxification in the marine aquarium, as opposed to a freshwater system, but also that there is less room for error. Marine fish are much less "forgiving" of sloppy aquarium man-agement, a fact that has caused many a novice aquarist much anguish as beautiful and costly specimens succumb because the aquarist tried to bend the rules. My advice is aimed at helping you avoid such mistakes. Stick to the rules until you have gained considerable experience.

A marine aquarium in your home can give you years of enjoyment and satisfaction. You can begin to design a marine aquarium right now, creating a miniature ecosystem that will thrive while enhancing your living space with some of the most spectacular examples of nature's marvelous diversity. Read, plan, shop carefully, ask questions, and make notes. Remember that in the fascinating hobby of marine aquarium keeping, patience is always amply rewarded.

THE CORAL REEF ENVIRONMENT

Successful marine aquarium design requires a thorough understanding of the natural environment you are trying to duplicate. Coral reefs and their adjacent environs offer living organisms an abundant diversity of habitat types.

Similar physical and chemical conditions prevail in the sea wherever coral reefs occur. One must create similar conditions in the aquarium as a prerequisite to keeping any reef-associated species. Three sets of environmental conditions, chemical, physical, and biological, must each be maintained within a specific set of ranges.

"Chemical conditions" refers to the concentrations of various ions that are dissolved in the water in the aquarium.

"Physical conditions" refers to parameters such as temperature, light intensity, light spectrum, photoperiod, currents, structure, and substrate.

"Biological conditions" are associated with the interactions among organisms in the same

Complex relationships characterize coral reefs. The anemone crab (Neopterolisthes maculatus) cannot survive away from its host anemone.

area. The latter types of conditions are the most complex, and we will be examining various examples of how the biological environment of the sea and your aquarium can be quite similar in some cases, and completely different in others. Chemical and physical parameters are more readily defined and manipulated than are innate patterns of fish behavior. This makes the aquarist's task both one of supplying the physical and chemical conditions found in a reef habitat and of accommodating each organism's unique biological requirements, as, for example, a particular type of food.

Seawater—The Chemical Environment

We learn early in life that seawater is salty, and that may be the full extent of our knowledge of the makeup of this unique substance. Seawater, however, is more than a simple solu-

The flame angelfish (Centropyge loriculus) usually adapts well to aquarium life. Other angelfish species may not.

tion of salt, or sodium chloride. All chemical elements are found in seawater. Only some of them, however, are of interest to the marine aquarist. When we speak of the elements in their dissolved state, we refer to them as ions.

Ions

There are 11 major ions, those present at a concentration of one part per million (ppm) or more, that comprise 99.9 percent of the dissolved substances in seawater. These are: chloride, sulfate, bicarbonate, bromide, borate, fluoride, sodium, magnesium, calcium, potassium, and strontium. The major ions are "conserved," meaning that, while the total amount of these ions can vary locally—the salinity of the water can be different in different locations—the relative proportions of the conserved ions remain constant. Thus, the gross chemical composition of seawater is constant everywhere in the sea.

Two other groups of ions are found in seawater. Minor ions are those that are present at a level greater than one part per billion (ppb), but less than one ppm. Trace ions are those that are present in concentrations less than one ppb. An important distinction between the major elements and the minor and trace elements is that while the major ions are conserved, and therefore unaffected by local conditions, the concentrations of minor and trace elements *are* affected by chemical or biological processes. This is why altering the concentrations of certain ions has definite biological effects. Much debate occurs in aquarium-keeping circles regarding the merits of adding supplements to maintain or exceed the natural concentration of certain minor and trace elements. It would appear, however, that regular partial water changes suffice to replenish all that needs replenishing. Testing accurately for trace and minor elements can pose a challenge. My advice: Focus on keeping the known important parameters in line, and let the experimenters worry about trace elements. Those parameters include temperature, salinity, pH, alkalinity, nitrogen compounds, phosphate, and calcium. Later in the book, I will describe how to manage aquarium chemistry.

Light—The Physical Environment

Coral reefs develop only under specific conditions; light, in particular, must reach the coral organisms, because all reef-building corals harbor photosynthetic, symbiotic algae, known to biologists as *zooxanthellae*. Reefs form only where water clarity is sufficient to allow adequate light penetration. Sediments, transported from the coastline by rivers, both reduce light penetration, and can smother and destroy corals. Clear, sediment free water is the primary physical requirement for the development of a coral reef. Temperature, water movement, and underwater topography all play a role as well.

Reefs develop primarily in areas where the water temperature averages in the mid-seventies. Inshore shallows, however, may become much warmer than this during the day, and then cool off again at night. Consequently, organisms from the lagoon may be more tolerant of temperature fluctuations than those from the outer reef, washed by the open sea. Similarly, the water in the lagoon is much less turbulent than on the outer face of the reef. Corals that require heavy wave action are seldom found growing alongside sea mats accustomed to the quiet waters of the lagoon. Substrate conditions can further subdivide a habitat. Organisms that attach themselves to a

Octopus (O. bimaculatus) *typically inhabit inshore areas among rocks. They must be isolated in a tank to themselves, lest they feed on tank mates.*

solid surface will be found in areas of the lagoon with a hard bottom of fossil coral. Other species are adapted to sitting upon, or burrowing within, sandy substrates. Currents determine the location of accumulations of sand, mud, or clean-scoured rocks, providing another example of the influence of water movement on the ecosystem.

Interactions—The Biological Environment

The biological structure of the reef ecosystem is the result of factors that students of coral reef biology have only begun to elucidate. Coral

The bright green color of the coral garden shown here results from pigments produced by their symbiotic zooxanthellae.

biologist J.E.N. Veron describes the pattern of interactions that leads to the characteristically high biodiversity of reefs.

"This diversity can only exist after a series of ecological balances is achieved: not only balances between the corals themselves, but between the corals and other organisms . . . [E]ach species has its own array of growth strategies, food requirements, and reproductive capacities. The net result of all these interactions and balances . . . is to make coral communities among the most diverse of any communities on earth."

Understanding that such a complex web of ecological interactions exists on the reef helps to explain why specific conditions have to be met in the aquarium. For the vast majority of species available to marine aquarium hobbyists, a single, basic set of parameters, easily achieved

with simple techniques, are sufficient for survival, growth, and often reproduction. Some desirable organisms, are, however, more demanding than others are. Large sea anemones, for example, require not only near-perfect water conditions, but bright, wide-spectrum illumination. The Mandarin Dragonet feeds only upon tiny, living crustaceans that it plucks from among rocks. It frequently starves rather than accept alternative foods. I like to call species with more demanding requirements the "pivotal species" in any aquarium design. When conditions in the aquarium are suitable for the pivotal species, it is a safe bet that less demanding tankmates will also be accommodated. Identifying a pivotal species in your aquarium stocking plan will simplify all the other aspects of designing the system.

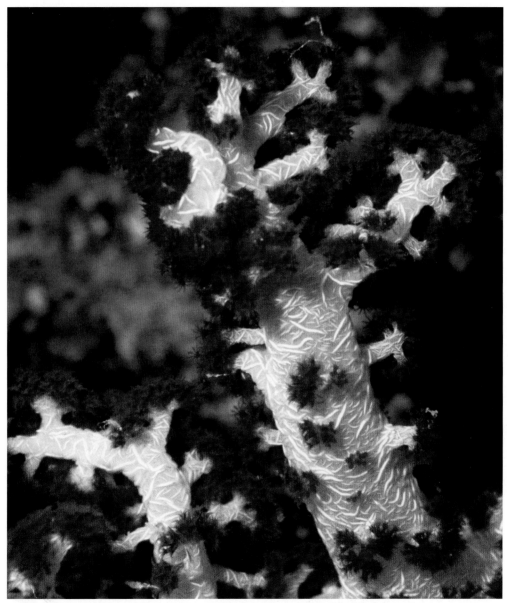

Corals of all types, such as the Tree Soft Coral (Dendronephthya klunzingeri) *shown here, will benefit from proper lighting, good water quality, and plankton substitutes.*

PLANNING YOUR AQUARIUM

Your goal as an aquarist should be for the fish and invertebrates in your aquarium to thrive, grow, and possibly reproduce themselves, living out a natural life span at least as long as the one they would have in the sea. To achieve this goal, you definitely need a plan.

Start creating a plan for your aquarium by purchasing a looseleaf binder, or setting up an "Aquarium" folder on your computer's hard drive. You will want to keep track of your ideas, and the information you collect as your plan develops. I suggest beginning your notebook by estimating the amount of time and money you are willing to devote to the aquarium. A marine aquarium requires conscientious maintenance. Therefore, you must set aside about an hour a week for aquarium chores, plus a few minutes twice a day for feeding and a quick checkup. You will also need to spend about half a day once a month for a major tuneup. I have found the time spent changes little up to about 100 gallons (378 L) of tank capacity. For a larger tank, the effort can be significantly greater. If you cannot spare

Providing for the needs of specialized feeders like this cowfish (Lactoria cornuta) should be part of the aquarium plan.

enough time for maintenance, the aquarium is doomed to failure unless you hire a service to do the work for you. Because this is a book intended for the rank beginner, a huge tank and professional maintenance are beyond its scope.

Size

The cost of an aquarium is, as you might expect, proportional to its size. While I recommend that your first marine aquarium be as large as possible, you will probably want to begin with a tank 4 feet (122 cm) long or smaller. This works out to about 75 gallons (284 L) for the upper end of the size range. In no case do I suggest you begin with an aquarium smaller than 20 gallons (76 L). "Micro-tanks" abound, and are undeniably cute, but wait until you have some experience before attempting to maintain one. A larger volume of water resists temperature fluctuation and can sustain more livestock than a smaller one.

An anemone shrimp (Periclimenes brevicarpalis) *and its host can be accommodated in a 20-gallon aquarium.*

Itty-bitty aquariums require constant attention to remain hospitable to their inhabitants.

Cost

For a complete 20-gallon (76 L) marine aquarium, including some moderately priced fish, expect to spend around $500. A 75-gallon (284 L) system with light-requiring invertebrates (discussed below) can run up a bill of $5,000. Besides the initial cost, there are monthly maintenance costs to consider. These include the cost of food, seawater, and items that require regular replacement, such as fluorescent lamps. Maintenance costs increase, of course, in proportion to the size of the aquarium.

Lighting

Let's say you've settled on a 30-gallon (113 L) tank. You must next decide if you want light-requiring invertebrates as part of your display. Numerous types of marine invertebrates harbor symbiotic algae in their tissues. The algae obtain certain nutrients from their hosts, and in turn provide "services," including nutrient recycling and an assist with the deposition of the host's calcium carbonate skeleton (if it has one). The corals that actually construct reefs all have symbiotic algae, technically known as *zooxanthellae*. Without the zooxanthellae, the coral cannot survive. Hence, aquarium lighting must cater to the needs of these microscopic algae. Most aquarium kits come with a single fluorescent lamp in a long, narrow fixture. You will need much more light than this for the 30-gallon (113 L) tank in our example. The tank is 3 feet (91 cm) long, allowing for a 30-watt fluorescent lamp to be accommodated along its length. For photosynthetic invertebrates, you should have

An exquisitely colored Helfrich's dartfish (Nemateleotris helfrichi).

Firefish (Nemateleotris magnifica) *spend much of their time out in the open. Hiding would be a sign of trouble in this species.*

at least two, and preferably four, 30-watt fluorescent lamps. The cost of an appropriate fixture for this many lamps increases the cost of the setup considerably. In addition, the lamps will require annual replacement.

Theme

I find it helpful to decide on a theme for the aquarium, then build the design around that. I have taken this approach to develop the examples provided later in the book. Choose a theme you can state in a single sentence: "My new aquarium will depict an outer reef slope in the Caribbean." Once you have the theme nailed down, you can choose possible aquarium inhabitants. Go through some references and make a list of fish and invertebrates that appeal to you. You will want to make note of their anticipated adult size, any special food demands, and so on. Getting this information together at the outset can spare you a huge amount of trouble later. You don't want to discover, for example, that the colorful baby damselfish you brought home six months ago is now becoming a drab, gray,

and obnoxiously aggressive adult. Narrow down your list to a few must-haves before you proceed further.

What Should You Buy?

Armed with a list of fish and/or invertebrates, you are ready to head for the shop to purchase your new aquarium tank and equipment. What should you buy? Over the years, aquarists, both amateur and professional, developed several methods for maintaining aquariums of coral reef organisms. These methods can be identified by their point of origin. Thus, we have designs from Berlin, the Smithsonian Institution, and the national aquarium of Monaco. The Berlin design relies upon live rock (discussed later, page 48) and the relatively simple technique of protein skimming to maintain water quality. Calcium is added to the aquarium along with evaporation makeup water, to provide for the construction of coral skeletons. Sometimes, additional supplements are added to the water. In the design developed at the Smithsonian,

The pajama cardinalfish (**Sphaeramia nematoptera**) *has been popular with saltwater hobbyists for years.*

in a ceaseless cycle of chemical conversions. Via photosynthesis, the zooxanthellae take part in the process of biochemical cycling, as do algae. Microscopic algae as well as the larger forms we call "seaweeds" absorb not only nitrogenous wastes but also carbon dioxide, and release oxygen into the water. All the aquarist really has to do is keep the water conditions within optimal range, and the life forms do the rest.

Note: Having said all that, I do suggest installing a protein skimmer on your first marine aquarium. This device removes organic matter in the form of a viscous, greenish brown liquid you can actually see in the collection cup. Simple in design and nearly foolproof, a skimmer provides an extra measure of insurance against declining water conditions. Beginners should find one well worth the additional up front investment.

water pollution control becomes the responsibility of an "algal turf scrubber" rather than a protein skimmer. In the Monaco system a partitioned, double layer of sand plays this role.

All three systems share more similarities than differences. All supply bright light for the zooxanthellae. All include live rock. All include a layer of coarse sand on the bottom of the tank. It turns out that these three elements, coupled with water movement, are all you really need. Even a simple system can be quite successful. As a beginner, you will appreciate that a simple system frees you to focus on the inhabitants rather than the technology. Why does a simple, "Natural Aquarium" work? Because the organisms on and within the live rock, and dwelling among the sand grains, carry out the same natural processes within the confines of the aquarium as they do in the sea. Microorganisms detoxify wastes and decompose organic matter

Philosophy of the "Natural" Aquarium

My approach to keeping marine organisms in captivity is really rather straightforward: duplicate nature in as many details as possible with techniques as simple as possible. Providing a physical and chemical environment closely similar to that found in nature is essential.

Nevertheless, one cannot reduce the dynamics of an ecosystem, even the small and relatively uncomplicated ecosystem of an aquarium, to a table of numerical parameters. The aquarist who nods in satisfaction at a pH reading within the correct range, yet fails to heed the message conveyed by a dying organism, is missing the point altogether. Beyond providing the correct parameters, you must attempt to duplicate the *biological* environment found on a real coral reef. You must begin the thinking process for the aquarium by asking questions about the needs of the species that will occupy it, and then design a system that provides for those needs, including such things as an appropriate social milieu, symbiotic partners, or living foods.

The tools you will need for creating a mini-reef aquarium of your own are provided throughout this book. It may be helpful in this regard to understand how the book is organized. The following chapters provide specific information about a selection of fish and invertebrates, together with a general discussion of fish families and invertebrate phyla. One section of this book is concerned with making appropriate combinations of species. These three chapters thus encompass the guidelines for structuring the biological environment of your mini-reef.

I discuss the actual process of setting up the aquarium in a step-by-step manner. Following these instructions should result in appropriate conditions for the initial physical and chemical environment of your captive reef. Once living organisms are added, these initial conditions will begin to change, however. Thus, "Caring for Your Aquarium" describes how to test the seawater in your aquarium, and how to make small adjustments when chemical conditions stray outside the target range. Feeding, the other major component of routine aquarium care, is also discussed in this chapter. Finally, "Troubleshooting" discusses common problems and their solutions.

Marine aquariums established by the methods outlined here are the most successful,

If you plan to keep pulse coral, such as this Xenia *species, tank conditions must be tailored to its needs.*

TIP

Coral

Sometimes, experienced aquarists discourage beginners from attempting an aquarium containing corals. But the principles of water-quality management are basically the same, whether the tank contains only fish, or whether it blossoms with coral polyps; therefore, go with whatever you like. Just remember—you will need to invest a bit more time and money on the latter type of aquarium, frequently known as a "minireef" or "reef tank."

easiest to maintain, and most likely to provide what species need to complete their life cycles. The basic features of these aquariums are: (1) ample quantities of "live rock" and "live sand," (2) high-intensity, broad-spectrum lighting, and a natural photoperiod, (3) protein skimming, to achieve removal of organic wastes rather than mineralization of them, (4) husbandry efforts focused upon maintaining physical and chemical conditions found in the sea, especially limiting quantities of inorganic nutrient ions, while providing a continuous supply of other inorganic ions in concentrations that match or exceed those found in the ocean, (5) replication of the physical characteristics of a specific microhabitat, in terms of substrate, currents, and structure, and (6) attention to the specific community and social relationships of the species housed together in the same aquarium.

By following the approach detailed here, you can create a thriving, natural-looking aquarium that is relatively easy to maintain.

The equipment you require—lights, pumps, protein skimmers, and timing devices—is uncomplicated in both design and operation. The essential biological elements, live rock and live sand, are interesting in their own right, and add to the aquarium a touch of realism that artificial decorations or the bleached skeletons of dead corals cannot convey.

Choosing a Dealer

"Success" with a marine aquarium can be defined as having fish and invertebrates that live as long as, or longer than, they would in the natural environment of the coral reef. In many cases, a major factor in achieving such success is the state of health of the organisms when you buy them. Therefore, choosing a dealer is an important aspect of managing your aquarium. Here are some suggestions for making wise decisions in this regard.

If you live in or near a reasonably large city, I suggest you start by looking for a store that sells only marine aquariums. Such a store can be expected to have a better selection, more knowledgeable personnel, and possibly better prices, than a store in which marine species are only a sideline. My second choice would be a shop that specializes in both freshwater and marine aquariums, and my third choice would be a full-line pet shop. Of course, there are good marine departments in stores that sell other kinds of pets, so this recommendation is made only to suggest a starting point for your investigations.

It is a good idea to make your first visit just an information-gathering trip; don't plan on buying fish for your tank on your first visit to any store. Furthermore, you should get a feeling for the range of offerings and stores in your region before making any decisions, especially if there are several competitors in a relatively

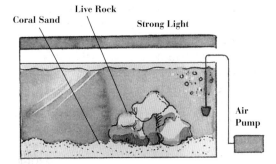

Coral Sand

Live Rock

Strong Light

Air Pump

Even a simple system with live rock can be successful.

Although the copperband butterflyfish (Chelmon rostratus) *often lives in pairs on the reef, two in the same aquarium will fight.*

small area. Make several visits a week or more apart. The idea is to find out how the store operates on a continuing basis. Be critical, but fair in your evaluations—bear in mind that we all have our good days and bad ones. I suggest visiting during a slow sales period, such as a weekday afternoon. This will give you a chance to learn more, because the staff will have more time to talk. Introduce yourself to the owner or the manager of the marine department, if possible. It is a good plan to have some specific questions in mind, for which you already know the correct answers, that you can ask in order to ascertain the level of knowledge of the people

with whom you speak. Do not expect everyone to be an infallible expert, but you should hear at least reasonably correct answers to basic questions about water quality, the particular needs (feeding behavior, for example) of any fish in the shop, and steps to prevent or cure the common parasitic infestations. One sign to watch for: when someone does not know the answer to your question, they take the time to look it up. Good shops always have several well-used reference books behind the counter.

Expect that attempts will be made to sell you products or specimens; after all, the store is in business to make money. However, the sales pitch should not be the sole communication you have with the staff. Professional retailers know that the key to their business is having successful hobbyists for customers. You should be able to discern a sincere interest in your success as an aquarist from the conversations you may have in the store. This would include such things as, for example, steering you away from specimens that would be inappropriate for your tank because of size or compatibility problems, or, if you describe yourself as a beginner, your level of expertise. Remember, though, that most dealers will sell you anything you want if you insist.

Choosing Healthy Fish

Let's say that the dealer seems knowledgeable, your conversation goes well, and you feel that this may be the store that you are looking for. The next step is to evaluate the specimens themselves, and there are several things that you should consider.

The huma-huma triggerfish (Rhineacanthus aculeatus) *is one of many colorful specimens from Hawaii.*

━━━━━━ T I P ━━━━━━

Choosing Species

Continue to develop your plan by listing any important considerations applicable to the species you have chosen. For example, the royal grammas included in one of the design suggestions provided later get along just fine in a group. The strikingly similar royal dottyback, on the other hand, refuses to tolerate another of its species in the same tank. Make sure you account for such factors in your aquarium plan.

Quarantine

First, the retailer should hold all new arrivals for at least a week before releasing them; two weeks in holding would be better. If this is not the routine at the store you select, they should at least be willing to do so if you buy the organism. Marine fish in particular have a harrowing journey from the reef to the retailer, and require a period of rest and adjustment before they are sent home with a hobbyist. A few days, or just until the fish has had its first meal, is not enough time for recovery. If the dealer cannot, or will not, provide this kind of "quarantine" period, you should make plans well in advance to quarantine all specimens at home yourself. I suggest a minimum quarantine of two weeks.

It is not enough for the fish merely to be eating in captivity. Mishandled fish can experience delayed mortality even if they have resumed feeding. However, any fish should definitely be eating in the dealer's tank before you purchase it.

Hawaii supplies snowflake moray eels (Echidna nebulosa) to the aquarium trade.

Chemicals

Hobbyists are frequently concerned about the use of chemicals, in particular cyanide, to collect marine fish. While it is difficult to ascertain what the actual numbers might be, suffice it to say there is a good chance that fish from certain locations may have been harvested with cyanide; however, progress in this area has been made, and there are many more drug-free fish on the market now than, say, ten years ago.

Research (Hall and Bellwood, 1995) has shown that stress and starvation resulting from poor holding and handling has more to do with mortality of ornamental marine fish than any inherent delicacy of constitution. It is important for beginners to realize how crucial their specimens' state of health at the time of aquisition is to their success. All kinds of things influence

Potter's angelfish (Centropyge potteri) lives only in the Hawaiian Islands. It feeds mostly on filamentous algae.

the condition of the marine fish and invertebrates that reach your dealer's inventory from distant reefs. Fish may be caught by illegal or environmentally destructive methods. Shipments may be subject to airline delays, exposure to excessive heat or cold, or jostling by a careless cargo handler. The many hands in the chain of custody from reef to retailer can care for the inventory with outstanding devotion or utter indifference.

Reputation of Retailer

At every level in the chain from reef to retail, the most reliable indicator of healthy specimens is the reputation of the supplier. If a dealer whose reputation you trust buys fish from an importer with whom he has had good experience, and who, in turn, buys from collectors with a good track record, the result is the best possible state of health for the majority of fish that the retail dealer might offer for sale. Unfortunately, it is seldom possible for the hobbyist to know much about this chain of custody. For this reason, you must assume the responsibility for choosing specimens wisely, based on their outward appearance. Your prior experience with a particular dealer may also influence your

Though sometimes challenging to keep, many sea basses (**Pseudanthias ventralis**) *rank among the most beautiful marine species.*

choices. As with any situation where multiple businesses compete for a relatively small number of customers, aquarium dealers tend to specialize. One dealer will have great corals, for example, while another shop may be the only place in town to buy clownfish. As a beginner, you may want to stick with some species that typically fare extremely well in captivity.

Hawaiian fish are especially good choices. These include the Yellow Tang *(Zebrasoma flavescens)*, which occurs in many locations in the Indo-Pacific region. Virtually all specimens offered in the aquarium trade, however, are from Hawaii, because they occur there in large numbers. In addition, shipping from Hawaii to the mainland is relatively inexpensive and does not involve red tape, since it is interstate commerce. Other Hawaiian species include Potter's Angel *(Centropyge potteri)*, Vanderbilt's Chromis *(Chromis vanderbilti)*, and several desirable butterflyfish, such as the Raccoon *(Chaetodon lunula)*, Threadfin *(C. auriga)*, and Longnosed *(Forcipiger flavissimus)*.

Florida also supplies many good aquarium fish, such as the French Angelfish *(Pomacan-*

thus paru) and the Yellowhead Jawfish *(Opisthognathus aurifrons)*. Other good aquarium fish come from the Caribbean region. Species such as the Royal Gramma *(Gramma loreto)* and its cousin, the Black Capped Basslet *(G. melacara)*, are obtained in this manner. With the exception of large angelfish, which can be challenging to the most capable aquarist, I have noted few problems with Hawaii, Florida, or Caribbean specimens over the years, provided they are given proper care by the retailer and subsequently by the hobbyist.

Captive-Propagated Fish

Captive-propagated fish are among the best possible choices, especially for the beginning aquarium hobbyist. Many species of clownfish are available from hatcheries, along with several kinds of gobies and dottybacks. Dealers usually advertise that they have captive-propagated stock, but you should always inquire. Captive-bred specimens may be smaller than wild-caught counterparts, but will of course grow to the size typical for their species. In all cases, captive-bred fish acclimate better to aquarium conditions and have fewer problems than do similar specimens harvested from the wild. An increase in hobbyist demand for captive-bred marine fish would have a positive effect on the industry, and would result in more species being made available than at present.

Health

One should become familiar with the signs of poor fish health. These include rapid opercular movements, excessive hiding, ragged fins, and the presence of lesions, open wounds, or similar abnormalities. Healthy fish look healthy: their colors are bright, they search actively for food,

═══ CHECKLIST ═══

Obtaining Healthy Fish

To summarize, there are five basic rules for obtaining healthy fish:

1. Know your dealer.
2. Know which fish come from what areas of the world.
3. Be aware of problems with fish from certain areas.
4. Learn to recognize the signs of poor health.
5. Don't shop only for price.

The black-capped basslet (Gramma melacara) *adapts readily to aquarium life. Found only in deep water, this species commands a high price.*

and their fins are held erect. Look for signs of poor nourishment, such as a hollow belly or thinning of the musculature behind the head. When viewed head on, the fish should be convex in outline, not concave. The usual advice is to look for signs of disease when shopping for marine fish, and this is a good plan, although only a very foolish, or very busy, dealer will leave sick fish in his display tanks these days.

Price

Finally, we come to the controversial issue of price. Many factors will affect the retail price of marine aquarium fish. These include the species, source, size of the store, geographic location of the store, the nature of the store's competition, prevailing labor and other costs in the area, and so on. My only advice is this: *do not shop for price alone.* Common sense must play a role in your evaluation of the "worth" of a particular specimen. For example, if an individual animal is being offered at a price that is "too good to be

true," I suggest extreme caution. A cheap fish is no bargain if it only lives a week or two after you take it home. Once you find a dealer who consistently provides you with good-quality fish, your best bet is to support that dealer with your business, even if a particular specimen is a few dollars less across town.

Mail Order

What about mail order dealers? Good ones are better than many local shops. Otherwise, how would they manage to stay in business when customers must pay freight costs and have no opportunity to see the fish that they are buying? Shop owners often complain about mail order livestock suppliers, but the fact is that the customers would not buy live specimens by mail-order, if they were not frustrated with their local dealer.

WHO LIVES WITH WHOM?

Choosing an appropriate community of organisms for your marine aquarium is not always a simple matter. The goal is to carefully select several specimens that appeal to you and have them live together harmoniously in the same aquarium.

While the different species of fish and invertebrates that you see in aquarium shops may all be found living together in apparent harmony on the reef, once confined in the aquarium their interactions can range from benign indifference to vicious hostility. Therefore, one must carefully plan the aquarium community, taking into account the lifestyles and requirements of the proposed inhabitants.

The first question you must answer regarding the list of species that will live in your captive sea is "Do I want invertebrates in the tank?" While an invertebrate aquarium can be interesting and relatively simple to maintain, combining invertebrates and fish must be done with care, lest some inhabitants become food for others. On the reef, invertebrates such as

A coral grouper (Cephalopholis miniata) yawns as it waits in ambush for a smaller fish to swim by.

crustaceans and mollusks are important food sources for many kinds of fish. Obviously, one cannot keep predators and prey together. Let us assume for the moment that your first marine aquarium will be a fish-only system; this is what many hobbyists begin with, in fact. We will return to the issue of keeping fish and invertebrates together later in this chapter.

Size Considerations

Two major considerations apply in the selection of a compatible community of marine fish: adult size and typical disposition. Dealing with these concerns first simplifies the process of creating a list of potential tankmates, since you generally cannot manipulate the aquarium environment to "get around" these constraints. It should be immediately apparent that you should not select a species that will outgrow its quarters, although this is a common occurrence

Because they are scarce in nature, the Bangaii cardinalfish (Pterapogon kauderni) *should only be purchased from hatcheries.*

by novice aquarists. You hear all sorts of excuses: there were plans for a bigger tank that never happened, it was unexpected that the specimen would grow so quickly, or the curious fallacy that the size of the aquarium might somehow restrict the growth of the occupants. I've heard many of these stories while standing across the counter from a hobbyist who was in need of finding a home for an overgrown pet. Unfortunately, few shops are willing, or even able, to accept specimens that have become too large to be accommodated by their owners. For one thing, shops must allocate their holding space parsimoniously—there may simply be no room this week for an unanticipated arrival, especially a sizable one. For another, shopkeepers are often concerned that returned specimens may harbor disease problems that might spread to the other inventory. (You might assume that the risk of disease introduction would be no greater than that for new fish arriving from a wholesaler. In this regard, however, the shop's supplier is a known quantity; a customer, particularly in a large urban area, may not be.) Only the most generous shop owner would welcome

a specimen that was not purchased there initially, although this is a request that I have personally received many times.

If the shop won't take back the specimen, your other options may be limited. Public aquariums seldom accept such donations, for example. The only choices may be buying another tank or euthanasia. Better to avoid this problem altogether, and find out the maximum anticipated size of any fish you are considering. Seek out your dealer's recommendations concerning the range of sizes that are suitable for your aquarium. Above all, use common sense. A fish that will reach 12 inches (30 cm) in length is a completely impractical choice for a 36-inch (90 cm) tank. Unless you have set up a rather large tank as a first effort, say more than 100 gallons (usually such a tank will be 6 feet long), it is best to limit yourself to fish species that grow no larger than about 3 to 6 inches, with the upper portion of this size range reserved for tanks that are at least 4 feet long. Doing so will not limit your choices all that much; there are scores of species from which to select. Remember that choosing specimens of suitable size for your tank will mean that their chances of living out a normal lifespan under your care will be greatly enhanced. Here are some rough guidelines:

For tanks 3 feet (90 cm) in length or smaller, choose from the following families: basslets, dottybacks, clownfish, some damselfish, dwarf angelfish, some hawkfish, dragonets, blennies, gobies, jawfish, and cardinalfish. For tanks from 3 to 6 feet in length, the choices expand to include wrasses, butterflyfish, and tangs, along with anthias and comet groupers, and some scorpionfish, eels, rabbitfish, puffers, triggerfish, and boxfish. Tanks more than 6 feet (1.8 m) in length could hold a larger community of any of these, and are essential for large angelfish, groupers, and triggerfish, or any species that reaches more than 1 foot (30 cm) in length, eels excepted.

Temperament

Having made a list of potential inhabitants that will not outgrow your proposed aquarium tank, you next must consider the typical disposition of species within the families you have selected. The various species of coral reef fish exhibit a range of behavioral specializations, because natural selection has favored those behaviors leading to survival and reproductive success. One can do little, therefore, to alter these innate patterns. One can, however, choose species whose typical behavior will not create conflicts in the captive community.

Some fish, for example, are intolerant of living with others of their own kind. Families in which this behavior is common (with occasional exceptions) include dottybacks, dragonets, hawkfish, groupers, triggerfish, large angelfish, and wrasses. The rules, however, are not absolute. Often, the gender of the fish determines whether it will tolerate others. Typically, male dragonets, wrasses, and both dwarf and large angelfish will not allow another male within sight, but all these males accept female companionship. In these families, females will usually, but not always, remain peaceful with each other.

Sea Basses

On the other hand, there are families in which the usual situation involves group living, and individuals deprived of an appropriate social milieu may not fare well. Certain species of sea basses are good examples. They normally live in shoals, and should be kept in groups of

Hermit crabs perform valuable services by scavenging for leftover food.

at least three individuals, preferably five or more, in the aquarium. Each shoal is dominated by a mature male, and consists of females and juvenile males that swim below him in the water column. The fish feed on plankton in open water. The hierarchy of the shoal apparently serves as protection from predators, to which the group is fully exposed. When some-

*Small, colorful gobies make good aquarium pets, like this limestriped sharp-nosed goby (***Elacatinus multifasciatum***).*

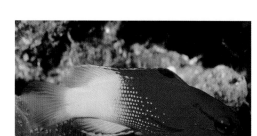

Beautiful royal grammas (**Gramma loreto**) *have helped introduce many a beginner to marine aquarium keeping.*

Tangs

Most tangs are shoaling fish, and while gender apparently does not determine dominance, these fish nevertheless exhibit a hierarchy, or "pecking order." The implications for aquarium care are straightforward: keeping two fish together will result in one individual's being constantly harassed by the other. Constant harassment of this sort will eventually cause the poor creature to die of starvation or disease. Keeping a group together, mimicking the natural pattern, spreads the aggression among several fish and no one specimen takes all the heat. Some species of tangs are so aggressive that they are intolerant of others of their kind, unless the group consists of a great many individuals. Keeping a large shoal is usually impossible for the typical hobbyist, so one is restricted to a single specimen. The Powder Blue Tang *(Acanthurus leucosternon)* is a good example of a species that must be kept singly, although it occurs in huge shoals in the Indian Ocean. Tangs are suitable only for larger aquariums. Their frequent confinement in tanks of less than 6 feet (185 cm) in length may be one reason why this family of herbivorous grazers is widely regarded as especially susceptible to parasitic infestations and disease in captivity.

thing happens to the dominant male, one of the younger males takes his place. Sea basses begin life as females and develop into males as they mature, a characteristic found in several types of marine fish, and known as *protogynous hermaphroditism*. The juvenile males, actually females approaching maturity, resemble younger females in color and finnage. When the dominant male dies, the changes that occur in the appearance of the juvenile male who succeeds in taking his place can be quite dramatic. In the aquarium, sea basses such as these often fail to eat and slowly starve, if they are deprived of the security of the shoal.

Dwarf Angelfish

Harem formation can be important to a fish's well-being. Dwarf angelfish *(Centropyge)* are similar to sea basses in that the younger specimens are all females that eventually mature into males. One male typically has a harem of several females within his territory, and

Who could resist the droll appearance of the longnosed hawkfish (**Oxycirrhites typus**)?

The flame hawkfish (**Neocirrhites armatus**) *will allow no other hawkfish to share its tank.*

Given a large tank, the foxface (**Lo vulpinus**) *can reach a foot in length and live for many years, feeding solely on seaweed and vegetable matter.*

excludes all other males. Duplicating this social structure in the aquarium not only leads to a peaceable community, it generally rewards the aquarist with the opportunity to watch the spawning behavior of the angelfish, which may occur at dusk almost every day.

Butterflyfish

Some fish need to be paired with a single mate to thrive. Most butterflyfish, for example, travel only in pairs. These may not be reproductive pairings, however, as two males or two females may form a bond. This behavior probably evolved to provide security as the fish forage along the reef. Exceptions exist, of course. The Copperband Butterflyfish *(Chelmon rostratus)* will not permit another of its species to live in the same aquarium. Various Pennant Butterflyfish *(Heniochus* sp.) form shoals, and so do better in captivity if a group shares the same tank. Like tangs, the butterflyfish family has a reputation for being difficult to keep. However, in the case of many butterflyfish species, nutritional specialization as well as a need for a large territory together pose significant obstacles to successful captive husbandry.

Other Species

Several fish species, such as the Signal Goby *(Signigobius biocellatus),* are virtually always found as mated pairs in the ocean, and do poorly in the aquarium if kept without a mate. Always seek out information regarding such specifics for any species you are considering. If your dealer cannot provide the details, check one of the references included at the end of this book before purchasing any unfamiliar fish.

Predators

Some fish are so aggressive that they may pose a threat to any tankmate that is not similarly robust. In this category are big predators—scorpionfish, groupers, eels, and triggerfish—along with the small, but spunky, damselfish. Scorpionfish, groupers, and eels usually express their aggressive tendencies only toward potential food items. Many of them eat other fish. Others specialize in certain invertebrates, usually mollusks or crustaceans. Do not make the mistake of relying on specialized feeding habits to permit you to "get away with" keeping these specimens with inap-

Lionfish (**Pterois volitans**) *make hardy aquarium specimens. Because of their venomous spines, they should not be kept when children are around.*

propriate companions. Some eels feed largely on cephalopods, such as octopus, for example, but will adapt the menu to include their neighbors if necessity demands it.

Triggerfish can be aggressive just for the heck of it. Some individuals may be so intolerant of any companionship that keeping them in solitary confinement is the only option. These fish

The regal tang (**Paracanthurus hepatus**) *lives in dense coral stands, and should be given a coral head to hide in.*

may also rearrange the tank decorations to suit themselves. While they can be amusing pets that demonstrate remarkable intelligence, triggerfish should be included in a community aquarium only with great caution. There are a few species, such as the Bluethroat Triggerfish *(Xanthichthys auromarginatus)* that are not so temperamental and can be kept in a community tank. Others, such as the Undulated Triggerfish *(Balistapus undulatus)* may attack anything that moves, including the aquarist's fingers. Do your homework before succumbing to the temptation to purchase these fish, despite their undeniable beauty.

For achieving maximum aggressiveness per unit of body size, no marine fish can match certain members of the damselfish family. This large group of generally hardy species exhibits a variety of lifestyles. However, several species often found available in aquarium shops are quite territorial. For example, the Domino Damselfish *(Dascyllus trimaculatus)* occupies a single coral head and will defend this territory unto death, even attacking fish much larger than itself should they stray too close. Keeping this damselfish often results in disappointment to novice marine aquarists because unfortunately too many dealers recommend establishing the biological filter by adding a damselfish or two. Aside from being a less-than-satisfactory way to initiate appropriate bacterial growth in the system, after the fish has occupied the aquarium alone for a month (the usual time needed for filter development) it comes to regard the entire tank as its exclusive domain, with disastrous consequences for any newcomer that the aquarist might subsequently introduce. (Adding ammonia in chemical form along with live rock is a better way to "seed" the system with a beneficial bacterial community.)

Fish and Invertebrates Combined

Lest I give the impression that creating a compatible community of marine fish is impossible, I will conclude this discussion with a list of families that are, generally speaking, compatible with each other. These families also happen to be good choices for inclusion in a tank featuring invertebrates. Further, since most are small, they can easily be accommodated in tanks of 50 gallons (189 L) or less. Even better, many are available from hatcheries, and are therefore less expensive and better adapted to aquarium life than their wild-caught counterparts. An occasional caveat is mentioned in connection with some families, and I have provided for each family some suggestions for species that are normally available in the aquarium trade. A selection of these is discussed in detail in the following chapter.

Clownfish and Damselfish (Pomacentridae)

Clownfish are damselfish that live in association with certain species of sea anemones in the ocean, but may be kept without them in the aquarium. Most popular is the Common Clownfish *(Amphiprion ocellaris)*. Other good choices are Clark's Clownfish *(A. clarki)*, Tomato Clownfish *(A. frenatus)*, and Maroon Clownfish *(Premnas biaculeatus)*. The latter is available in

Pygmy angelfish (Centropyge argi) *form harems and may be kept in a small group in the aquarium.*

two color varieties, one with white stripes on a maroon background, and the other with bright yellow stripes. Both are handsome fish.

Typically, a family group consisting of a large female, a smaller male, and several juveniles shares a single anemone. One should duplicate this arrangement in the aquarium. Since clownfish change sex from male to female as they mature, placing a group of juveniles together results in the fish sorting themselves out into the natural pattern with time. One individual will grow much larger than the others, becoming

It's hard to beat the orange-tailed blue damselfish (Chrisyptera cyanea) *for both hardiness and breathtaking colors.*

No doubt about it, the common clownfish (**Amphiprion ocellaris**) *is the most popular aquarium fish of all.*

the female. Her presence will inhibit the development of the remainder, although the most robust of these will become the functional male. The only problem one might encounter with clownfish is in attempting to keep different species together in the same aquarium. This will work only while all fish are juveniles. As they mature, interspecific aggression will become quite severe. (For more detailed information on this remarkable group of fish, see my book,

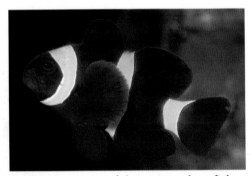

In most specimens of the maroon clownfish (**Premnas biaculeatus**) *the stripes are white, but some individuals have bright yellow stripes.*

Clownfish and Sea Anemones in the Home Aquarium, also from Barron's.)

Although some can become quite aggressive depending upon species and tank conditions, as described above, damselfish offer the hobbyist some of the hardiest possibilities for tank inhabitants. Perhaps the best choice is the Orange-Tailed Blue Damselfish *(Chrysiptera cyanea).* Only the mature male fish has the orange tail, which nicely complements his electric blue body color. Females and juveniles are completely blue, with a black dot at the base of the dorsal fin. These fish are found in shallow lagoons, where the male guards a territory shared by his harem. Creating an aquarium for this species alone, together with an assortment of the invertebrates that also live in the lagoon, results in an almost foolproof miniature ecosystem.

Fairy Basslets (Grammidae)

Fairy basslets are all cave or ledge-dwellers that occupy deeper waters on the fore reef in the Caribbean. The Royal Gramma *(Gramma loreto)* is usually stocked by dealers. It lives in groups in the ocean, although males may fight in the aquar-

Like all clownfish, the tomato clown (**Amphiprion frenatus**) *can live for 15 years in the aquarium.*

Though expensive, the swissguard basslet (**Liopropoma rubre**) *thrives under aquarium conditions.*

ium. To avoid this, select smaller individuals, which are more apt to be female. Otherwise, the species is nonaggressive, and a good choice for a mini-reef with a Caribbean theme.

Sea Basses (Serranidae)

Many smaller sea basses, as mentioned earlier, are shoaling fish. A solitary form from deep water, the Sunburst Anthias *(Serranocirrhitus latus)* is an excellent choice for the community aquarium, however, although beginning hobbyists can find it too expensive. The exquisite Longfin Anthias *(Pseudanthias ventralis hawaiiensis)* is a good choice for a shoaling anthias. Males are adorned with lovely streamers extending from the pelvic and anal fins. Their coloration is hot pink, with a yellow head and purple caudal fin, while females are yellow, with lavender sides. This fish lives at depths of more than 100 feet (30 m), and must be carefully decompressed as it is brought to the surface or it will not fare well subsequently. (The wise hobbyist will purchase this species only from a trusted source.) Once properly accli-

mated, however, it is easily maintained. As with many deepwater fish, *P. ventralis* will take a variety of foods. It grows only to about 3 inches (7.6 cm), and should be kept in a harem consisting of one male and several females.

Some of the other members of the often-predatory sea bass family are suitable for the community aquarium. The Belted Sandfish *(Serranus subligarius)* reaches only 3 inches (7.6 cm), and so poses no threat to any fish or crustacean it cannot swallow. More exotic is the Swissguard Basslet *(Liopropoma rubre)*, which lives in deeper waters. Despite its beauty, its

Clark's clownfish (**Amphiprion clarkii**) *comes in many color variants.*

A neon dottyback (Pseudochromis aldabraensis) is ever on the alert for food.

The sunrise dottyback (Pseudochromis flavivertex) is one of many dottybacks now being bred in captivity.

rather high cost may deter beginning aquarists, although it is an excellent choice.

Dottybacks (Pseudochromidae)

Most of the common species of dottybacks are now available from hatchery production. Only one tolerates its own kind. This is the Orchid Dottyback *(Pseudochromis fridmani)*, native to the Red Sea. For the remainder, such as the brilliant blue and orange Neon Dottyback *(P. aldabraensis)*, it is one to a customer unless

a mated pair can be obtained. All these fish remain under four inches in length.

Hawkfish (Cirrhitidae)

Only two hawkfish species should be considered for the community aquarium, although both are quite desirable. The Flame Hawkfish *(Neocirrhites armatus)* is perhaps a better selection than the Longnose Hawkfish *(Oxycirrhites typus)* only because the latter has a larger mouth and bigger appetite. Neither gets very large however, about 3 inches (7.6 cm) maximum, and both perch in coral heads or on other objects in a delightful

Like other hawkfishes, the pixie hawkfish (Cirrhitichthys falco) surveys everything from its perch.

Related to sea basses, the blue assessor (Assessor macneili) is a good choice for a beginner with a 30-gallon tank.

way that suggests they are overseeing all events that take place within the tank.

Cardinalfish (Apogonidae)

The cardinalfish family received rather little attention from aquarium hobbyists, until the spectacular Banggai Cardinalfish *(Pterapogon kauderni)* was introduced to the aquarium community a few years ago by Dr. Gerald Allen. Cardinalfish are often nocturnal, although this is not the case with *P. kauderni*. They all remain rather small, and feed on plankton or small crustaceans such as shrimp. They are not often seen in aquarium shops, but any species you do encounter is worth investigating as a potential member of your aquarium community.

Blennies (Blenniidae)

The often droll-looking blennies are either vegetarians or mid-water plankton feeders. A good choice among the latter group is the Canary Blenny *(Meiacanthus oualanensis)*. This species is bright yellow and is found only around the Fiji Islands. It ignores other fish as well as invertebrates. Another possibility are any of the Sailfin Blenny clan *(Acanthemblemaria* sp.) that will occupy holes in the rock and explode out like popcorn popping when food is added to the aquarium.

Dragonets (Callionymidae)

Only two species of dragonets are typically offered to aquarists, and both are quite spectacular in coloration. Dragonets should be kept only in an established aquarium with plenty of live rock,

Virtually all cardinalfish, such as this blue-striped cardinal (Apogon cyanosoma) *adapt to life in the aquarium.*

A queen angelfish (Holacanthus ciliaris) *demands a large aquarium and attentive care, and should be kept only by those with experience.*

If you have a large tank, a harlequin tuskfish (Choerodon fasciatus) *makes a good choice. It feeds on a variety of seafood fare.*

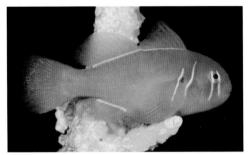

Coral gobies perch in coral heads. This is a citron coral goby (Gobiodon citrinus).

A green coral goby (Gobiodon histrio) *seldom grows larger than 1½ inches.*

as they feed only on tiny benthic invertebrates. Such food organisms will grow naturally in a thriving mini-reef. When their requirement for appropriate food is met, the Mandarin *(Synchiropus splendidus)* and the Spotted Mandarin *(S. picturatus)* are ideal specimens for a reef tank. In all dragonets, the male can be distinguished from the female by the greatly elongated first spine of the dorsal fin, and by his larger size. One can keep mandarins of the same species together as trios consisting of one male and two females. One can also keep the two mandarin species together, but one should never put two male mandarins of the same species together. They will fight until one is killed. Mandarins are seldom bothered by other fish, perhaps because they are poisonous if eaten. They ignore other tank occupants, apart from their tiny food sources.

Jawfish (Opistognathidae)

The most readily available species from the jawfish family is the Yellowheaded Jawfish *(Opistognathus aurifrons)* from Florida and the Caribbean. Yellowheaded Jawfish can be kept singly or in groups (a group is more fun to watch) in any size aquarium that will accommodate the number of fish desired. They will exca-

vate vertical burrows in the substrate, about twice as deep as the fish is long, so the aquarium must contain a deep layer of sand, shells, and pebbles. Jawfish feed on planktonic organisms snatched from the water column, and accept a variety of fresh and/or frozen foods.

Dartfish (Microdesmidae)

The dartfish family includes the fire gobies and torpedo gobies. The Common Fire Goby *(Nemateleotris magnifica)* from several locations in the Indo-Pacific region, has a cream-colored body, with a brilliant flame red tail. It hovers in midwater with its elongated dorsal fin held erect. The Blue Gudgeon *(Ptereleotris microlepis)* is typical of torpedo gobies. It is an elongated species, baby blue with a single black splotch in the fork of the tail. This species will spend more time out in the open if kept in a group; singles often hide. They do not squabble among themselves, as is sometimes the case with fire gobies.

Gobies (Gobiidae)

The Neon Goby *(Elacatinus oceanops)* was among the first marine fish to be spawned in captivity, and today, thousands of them are reared for the aquarium trade. Just over 1 inch

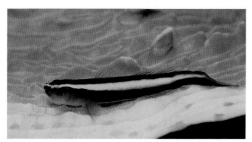

Many sharp-nosed gobies (**Elacatinus oceanops**) *remove parasites from other fishes, but will accept traditional aquarium foods, too.*

(2.5 cm) in length, black in color with brilliant blue and white horizontal stripes, the Neon Goby is at home even in a small tank. Related species, the Green-Banded Goby *(E. multifasciatus),* the Red-Headed Goby *(E. puncticulatus),* and the Citron Goby *(Gobiodon okinawae)* are now also available as captive propagated specimens. Gobies, in general, remain small in size, are easy to feed, and are nonaggressive.

Tangs (Acanthuridae)

While keeping tangs can sometimes pose problems, they are hardy if their needs are understood, and make good choices for the larger community aquarium. As described earlier, tangs should either be kept as solitary specimens, or in groups of at least three individuals. Solitary tangs are more likely to be aggressive to other fish. They must also be given a large tank, at least 4 feet (122 cm) in length. Among the best of choices is the Yellow Tang *(Zebrasoma*

*The fascinating relationship between certain gobies and snapping shrimps can be observed in the aquarium (***Stonogobiops** nematodes *with shrimp* **Alpheus randallii**).*

flavescens), collected almost exclusively in Hawaii. Desjardin's Sailfin Tang *(Z. desjardinii),* found in the Red Sea, is another possibility. The most popular species, perhaps, is the Regal Tang *(Paracanthurus hepatus).* The former two species are largely vegetarian, while the latter feeds more commonly on plankton. The major drawbacks to keeping tangs in captivity are their large size (up to 6 inches [15 cm] for the species mentioned, and much larger for several others), a requirement for abundant algae on which the vegetarian species can constantly graze, and a tendency to develop common parasitic infestations when conditions are stressful. They require ample space.

Choosing a compatible community of coral reef fish is not straightforward, but do not despair. Even beginning hobbyists succeed in keeping several brilliantly colored species together in peaceful coexistence. The important thing is that the selection process consist of planning and research, not trial and error. The latter approach is certain to lead to disappointment, not to mention dead fish. The former approach requires only that one spend some time before spending money.

FISH AND INVERTEBRATES FOR THE BEGINNER

Anyone who has had the experience of working with living organisms knows that some species are more amenable to domestication than others are. In the plant kingdom, roses are fussier than dandelions, for example. The same principle holds true for marine fish and invertebrates.

In this chapter, I have chosen 25 species of fish and 25 species of invertebrates that I recommend for the beginning marine aquarium hobbyist. I have also provided a brief summary of how fish and invertebrates are classified. With this information, you should be able to look up more detailed data about any species of marine fish or invertebrate of interest.

Classification of Marine Organisms

Familiarity with scientific nomenclature will make locating facts about marine life much simpler, because common names may vary, but

Plan on a tank of at least 100 gallons to accommodate a French angelfish (Pomacanthus paru).

each species has only one scientific name. The scientific name consists of two parts. The genus name identifies a particular group of closely related species. Most clownfish, for example, belong to the genus *Amphiprion*. However, the fish commonly called "Maroon Clownfish" is placed in the genus *Premnas*, because it differs from all other clownfish in having two spines on its gill covers rather than only one.

The second part of the scientific name is the species name. For example, the Common Clownfish is *Amphiprion ocellaris*. A related clownfish, the Percula Clownfish, is *Amphiprion percula*. These two species differ in minor structural details that are not readily apparent to the average aquarist. They are so similar in outward appearance that the name "Percula Clownfish" has been applied incorrectly to *A. ocellaris* almost universally in the aquarium trade for perhaps 30 years.

Taxonomic List of Recommended Marine Aquarium Fish

Scorpionfish, Scorpaenidae
   Pterois sphex, Hawaiian Lionfish
   Dendrochirus barberi, Hawaiian Turkeyfish
Sea Basses, Serranidae
   Serranocirrhitus latus, Sunburst Anthias
   Liopropoma rubre, Swissguard Basslet
Fairy Basslets, Grammidae
   Gramma loreto, Royal Gramma
   Gramma melacara, Blackcap Basslet
Dottybacks, Pseudochromidae
   Pseudochromis aldabraensis, Neon Dottyback
   Pseudochromis fridmani, Orchid Dottyback
Cardinalfish, Apogonidae
   Pterapogon kauderni, Bangaii Cardinalfish
Hawkfish, Cirrhitidae
   Oxycirrhites typus, Long-Nosed Hawkfish
   Neocirrhites armatus, Flame Hawkfish
Damselfish, Pomacanthidae
   Premnas biaculeatus, Maroon Clownfish
   Amphiprion clarkii, Clark's Clownfish
   A. ocellaris, Common Clownfish

   A. frenatus, Tomato Clownfish
   Chrysiptera cyanea, Orange-Tailed Blue Damselfish
Angelfish, Pomacanthidae
   Centropyge potteri, Potter's Dwarf Angelfish
   C. argi, Pygmy Dwarf Angelfish
Gobies, Gobiidae
   Elacatinus oceanops, Neon Sharp-Nosed Goby
   Elacatinus multifasciatus, Limestriped Sharp-Nosed Goby
   Gobiodon citrinus, Citron Coral Goby
   Gobiodon rivulatus, Green Striped Coral Goby
   Amblygobius rainfordi, Rainford's Goby
Dragonets, Callionymidae
   Synchiropus splendidus, Mandarin Dragonet
Jawfish, Opistognathidae
   Opistognathus aurifrons, Yellow-Headed Jawfish

That species can be distinguished on the basis of seemingly trivial differences is a source of annoyance to some hobbyists. However, the real distinction between two species that are otherwise nearly identical is that they do not interbreed in their natural environment. Other differences, such as those between the two species of clownfish, are secondary, but useful in assigning a particular specimen to one species or another.

A species is identified by the combination of genus and species name, as in *Amphiprion ocellaris*. Scientific names are always printed in italics. The genus name is always capitalized; the species name never is. The genus name can stand alone to refer to all species included within the genus. The species name, by itself, is meaningless.

Just as related species are grouped into genera, so related genera are grouped into families. Clownfish, thus, are grouped with the genera *Pomacanthus, Chromis, Dascyllus, Chrysiptera*, and several others into the damselfish family, formally known as the Pomacanthidae. Family names are capitalized, end in "-idae," and are not printed in italics. Learning about marine aquarium fish by families has proven to be the simplest approach for most beginners. Family relationships among marine fish often reflect important similarities in lifestyle.

Sea urchins and other grazing invertebrates help to keep algae growth under control.

Marine Fish Families

Each of the species mentioned in the listing below can successfully be maintained for the duration of its normal lifespan in an aquarium of 30 gallons (113 L) established and maintained by the methods described in this book. The sole exception is the Hawaiian Lionfish, which will eventually require a 50-gallon (189 L) tank. While two or more of the smaller species, gobies, for example, might be combined within the same 30-gallon (113 L) tank, having a community of more than two or three fish will require a bigger aquarium. For each species in the list, its adult size, food preferences, habitat preferences, and other pertinent information are given in Tables 1 and 2.

Marine Invertebrate Phyla

All fish, all vertebrate animals, in fact, belong to the same phylum, Chordata, or the chordates. Phyla are groups of organisms thought to share a common, and very old, evolutionary lineage. While the characteristics that biologists use to recognize phyla are beyond the scope of this book, it is convenient to use this classification scheme when discussing invertebrates. Invertebrates comprise roughly 95 percent of the animal kingdom, and exhibit enormous diversity. Some 30 invertebrate phyla are recognized. With the exception of the representatives of some minor phyla that one might find growing on a piece of live rock, there are only five invertebrate phyla of interest to the marine

Table 1
Suggested Stocking Levels, Adult Size, and Social Requirements
for 25 Species of Marine Fish

Common Name	Number/ 30 gal.	Adult Size (in.)	Social Requirements
Potter's Angelfish	3	4	Solitary or harem
Pygmy Angelfish	3	$2^3/4$	Solitary or harem
Bangaii Cardinalfish	3	3	Forms shoals
Common Clownfish	3	6	Family group
Maroon Clownfish	3	7	Family group
Orange-Tailed Blue Damsel	3	3	Harem
Tomato Clownfish	3	4	Family group
Clark's Clownfish	3	4	Family group
Neon Dottyback	1	$3^1/2$	Solitary or mated pair
Orchid Dottyback	1	$3^1/2$	Solitary or mated pair
Mandarin Dragonet	3	4	Solitary or harem only, males fight
Royal Gramma	3	3	Solitary or harem
Blackcap Basslet	1	4	Solitary
Rainford's Goby	3	4	Solitary or group
Green-Striped Coral Goby	5	2	Solitary or group
Neon Sharp-Nosed Goby	5	2	Solitary or group
Limestriped Sharp-Nosed Goby	5	2	Solitary or group
Citron Coral Goby	5	2	Solitary or group
Long-Nosed Hawkfish	1	5	Solitary, dislikes its own kind
Flame Hawkfish	1	3	Solitary, dislikes its own kind
Yellow-Headed Jawfish	3	4	Community group
Hawaiian Lionfish	1	10	Solitary or group
Swissguard Basslet	1	3	Solitary, dislikes its own kind
Sunburst Anthias	3	3	Solitary or harem

Table 2
Habitat and Feeding Preferences for 25 Species of Marine Fish

Common Name	Collected From	Habitat Preferences	Food
Potter's Angelfish	Hawaii (endemic)	Shallow reefs, common	Algae
Pygmy Angelfish	Florida and Caribbean	Deep reefs to reef tops, among rocks	Algae
Bangaii Cardinalfish	Indonesia	Grass beds	Small, meaty seafoods[1]
Common Clownfish	Indo-Australian	Shallow, exposed habitats	Small, meaty seafoods and algae
Maroon Clownfish	Indo-Australian	Deep outer reef slope	Small, meaty seafoods and algae
Orange-Tailed Blue Damsel	Western Pacific	Shallow lagoons	Small, meaty seafoods and algae
Tomato Clownfish	Indonesia to Japan	Lagoons and reef tops	Small, meaty seafoods and algae
Clark's Clownfish	Persian Gulf to Micronesia	Many reef and near-reef habitats	Small, meaty seafoods and algae
Neon Dottyback	Persian Gulf	Among corals	Small, meaty seafoods
Orchid Dottyback	Red Sea	Among corals	Small, meaty seafoods
Mandarin Dragonet	Tropical West Pacific	Shallow lagoons, inshore reefs	Tiny, living crustaceans only
Royal Gramma	Caribbean	Deep outer reefs	Small, meaty seafoods
Blackcap Basslet	Caribbean	Deep outer reefs	Small, meaty seafoods
Rainford's Goby	West-Central Pacific	Inshore, over sandy or muddy bottoms	Tiny seafoods[2], and filamentous algae
Green-Striped Coral Goby	Indo-West Pacific	Among tabletop corals	Tiny seafoods
Neon Sharp-Nosed Goby	Florida and Caribbean	Forms "cleaning stations"	Tiny seafoods
Limestriped Sharp-Nosed Goby	Caribbean	Inshore shallows under shelter	Tiny seafoods
Citron Coral Goby	Indo-Pacific	Among branching corals	Tiny seafoods
Long-Nosed Hawkfish	Indo-Pacific	Outer reefs in strong currents	Small, meaty seafoods
Flame Hawkfish	Pacific	Outer reefs, among branching corals	Small, meaty seafoods
Yellow-Headed Jawfish	Florida and Caribbean	Near reefs, in sand or rubble	Small, meaty seafoods
Hawaiian Turkeyfish	Hawaii (endemic)	Shallows, among rocks	Crustaceans
Hawaiian Lionfish	Hawaii (endemic)	Shallows, caves, and ledges	Crustaceans
Swissguard Basslet	Caribbean	Deep outer reefs	Small, meaty seafoods
Sunburst Anthias	Indo-Australian	Caves on outer reefs	Small, meaty seafoods

[1]Small, meaty seafoods include adult brine shrimp, mysids, roe, and any fish, shellfish, or crustacean meat chopped into pieces of $^1/_4$ inch (6 mm) or less in size.
[2]Tiny seafoods include brine shrimp nauplii, copepods, and any fish, shellfish, or crustacean meat finely minced.

Taxonomic List of Recommended Marine Invertebrate Species

Phylum Cnidaria
  Soft Corals
    Green Star Polyp Soft Coral
    Sarcophyton, Leather Mushroom Soft Coral
  Sea Mats
    Yellow Colonial Polyp Sea Mat
  Disc Anemones
    Discosoma
    Rhodactis
  Stony Corals
    Trachyphyllia
  Sea Anemones
    Entacmaea quadricolor, Clownfish Host Anemone
    Condylactis gigantea, Florida Pink-Tipped Anemone
    Bartholomea annulata, Curlicue Anemone
Phylum Arthropoda
  Crustaceans
    Lysmata amboiensis, Scarlet Cleaner Shrimp
    Stenopus hispidus, Banded Coral Shrimp
    Hippolysmata wurdemanni, Peppermint Shrimp
    Clibanarius tricolor, Blue-Legged Hermit Crab
    Paguristes cadenanti, Scarlet Hermit Crab
    Alpheus armatus, Curlicue Snapping Shrimp
Phylum Mollusca
  Bivalves
    Tridacna maxima, Blue Giant Clam
    Tridacna derasa, Ponderous Giant Clam
    Tridacna gigas, Giant Giant Clam
  Snails
    Algae-eating snails
Phylum Echinodermata
  Sea Stars
  Brittle and Serpent Stars
  Sea Urchins
    Eucidaris tribuloides, Caribbean Slate Pencil Urchin
  Sea Cucumbers
    Colochirus robustus, Yellow Sea Cucumber
Phylum Annelida
  Fanworms
    Sabellastarte, Giant Feather Duster Worm

aquarist. These are corals and their relatives, crustaceans, snails and clams, sea stars and their kin, and segmented worms. These phyla are labeled, respectively, Cnidaria, Arthropoda, Mollusca, Echinodermata, and Annelida. Representatives of each of these groups that are good choices for a beginner's mini-reef are shown in the accompanying list. For each species, its food and habitat preferences and other pertinent information are provided in Table 3.

Live Rock

Live rock is usually dead coral skeletons or limestone from fossil coral reefs that is removed from the ocean with encrusting plants and animals attached. The nature of live rock can vary due to many factors, including the kind of rock, the collecting locality, the depth from which the rock is taken, the numbers and kinds of organisms present at the time of collection, the method of storage and transport between the collector and the hobbyist.

Among the sea basses, the sunburst anthias (Serranocirrhitus latus) *is a good choice for the novice.*

One of the best choices for beginners, the scarlet cleaner shrimp (Lysmata amboiensis) *adapts easily to aquarium life.*

Live rock is harvested from shallow, inshore areas of several Pacific island countries, notably Fiji, Tonga, and Samoa. Cultivation of live rock takes place in Florida under special permits. Live rock is cultivated in the central Gulf of Mexico, as well as in the Florida Keys.

Of utmost importance to the hobbyist is the treatment that the rock receives between collection and retail sale. You will generally be unable to obtain this information with certainty, and must rely on your experience with your dealer and the information he or she is able to provide concerning your live rock purchase.

The best live rock is "cured" before you purchase it. Collectors do not ship live rock in water. This is to minimize the cost of air freight, a substantial portion of the retail price. The degree to

Pennant butterflyfish (Heniochus acuminatus) *can be more easily fed than many other butterflyfish species.*

which the organisms that were originally present on the rock arrive intact in your aquarium depends upon how long the rock has been out of water on its journey to your aquarium.

Live rock is packed in wet newspaper, and shipped in insulated cartons. Despite these precautions, there will be a significant amount of die-off of the encrusting organisms. This die-off creates pollution, and generates large amounts of organic debris, when the rock is placed under

Table 3
Care, Feeding, and Habitat Preferences for 25 Marine Invertebrate Species

Common Name	Light?	Feed?	Food	Collected	Habitat
Mushroom Polyp	Y	Y	Plankton substitute	Indo-Pacific	Wide ranging, in indirect light and calm water
"Hairy" Blue Mushroom Polyp	Y	Y	Plankton substitute	Tonga	Partially shaded back reefs on dead coral branches
Leather Mushroom Soft Coral	Y	Y	Plankton substitute	Indo-Pacific	Shallow lagoons in turbid water
Yellow Polyp Sea Mat	Y	Y	Plankton substitute	Indonesia	Loose rubble on sand in bright, shallow areas
Green Star Polyp Soft Coral	Y	Y	Plankton substitute	Indonesia	Lagoons, bays, outer reef slope
Pink-Tipped Anemone	Y	Y	Small pieces of seafood	Florida	Grass beds, back reef flats
Bulb Anemone	Y	Y	Small pieces of seafood	Indonesia	Shallow lagoons, on rocks
Curlicue Anemone	N	Y	Small pieces of seafood	Florida	Grass beds, back reef flats
Open Brain Stony Coral	Y	Y	Plankton substitute	Indo-Pacific	Shallow lagoons, on mud or sand
Giant Feather Duster	N	N	Bacteria, plankton	Florida, Hawaii	Inshore, quiet waters
Star Shell	N	N	Algae films	Florida	Intertidal
Turban Shell	N	N	Algae films	Worldwide	Intertidal to subtidal
Blue Giant Clam	Y	N	Plankton substitute	Captive-propagated	Shallow water, embedded in rocks
Ponderous Giant Clam	Y	Y	Plankton substitute	Captive-propagated	Outer reefs, up to 60 ft.
Giant Giant Clam	Y	Y	Plankton substitute	Captive-propagated	Sand or rubble bottoms, up to 60 ft., grass beds
Scarlet Cleaner Shrimp	N	Y	Scavenger	Worldwide	Cleaning "stations" among corals
Scarlet Hermit Crab	N	N	Algae	Florida	Many near-reef and reef habitats
Banded Coral Shrimp	N	Y	Scavenger	Florida	On reefs at shallow to moderate depths
Blue-Legged Hermit Crab	N	N	Algae	Florida	Shallow, inshore areas among rocks
Peppermint Shrimp	N	Y	Scavenger	Florida	Shallow water among sponges and tunicates
Curlicue Shrimp	N	N	Scavenger	Florida	Associates with Curlicue Anemone
Caribbean Slate Pencil Urchin	N	Y	Algae, small pieces of seafood	Florida	On rocks in shallow to moderate depths
Yellow Sea Cucumber	N	Y	Plankton substitute	Indo-Pacific	Lagoons, shallow reefs
Brittlestar	N	N	Scavenger	Florida	Shallow water, among rocks
Serpent Star	N	N	Scavenger	Florida	Shallow water, among rocks

With proper attention to maintenance, even a beginner can create a beautiful miniature reef.

water once again. Curing must therefore take place in a container separate from the display aquarium.

As soon as rock is received from the supplier, it should be briefly rinsed in a bucket of seawater to dislodge any loose material, and immediately placed in holding tanks. There should be about 2 gallons (7 L) of water in the holding tanks per pound of live rock. The rock remains in the holding tanks for two weeks, or longer if necessary, to allow beneficial bacteria to restore the rock to health by breaking down dead organisms and replacing the original biomass of the rock with their own microscopic cells. In a well-seasoned curing system, an assortment of beneficial organisms may be "seeded" onto the

rock, resulting in a partial restoration of its original biodiversity. This community of organisms tends to become established naturally in the curing system over time. It results from a process of artificial selection: small invertebrates, and microorganisms able to survive and reproduce under conditions in the rock curing system flourish and are subsequently transferred to the display aquarium after curing, with obviously beneficial effects. When the curing process is complete, the rock has a fresh, "ocean" smell, and is free of dead, decaying organisms. Besides a thriving population of beneficial bacteria that have fed on the abundant nutrients released in the process of decay, the rock will have present numerous colonies of

Invertebrates that filter the water, such as this fanworm, require a plankton substitute in order to survive.

pink, mauve, and purple encrusting coralline algae. Cultivated live rock from the Gulf of Mexico may also have small stony coral colonies, which are legally available to hobbyists only if obtained attached to a piece of cultivated live rock. This rock often develops an assortment of green or red macroalgae growth that looks especially good if kept well-pruned by herbivorous fish. Few large organisms will be apparent immediately after curing, although the rock harbors spores, holdfasts, and other portions of organisms, from which new macroalgae, and sometimes invertebrates, will grow, once the rock becomes part of a maturing mini-reef. Sponges, tubeworms, and other small, encrusting organisms not at first apparent on freshly cured rock, often begin to regrow

after the completed mini-reef has had the opportunity to develop by itself for several months. From the details provided, it should be apparent that curing of live rock is a process best left to a dealer with a large system designed for the purpose. An intrepid hobbyist who undertakes the process at home experiences two major problems: (1) the home system must be temporary, all the rock needed is cured at once and there is no further use for the system; (2) there is no established population of beneficial organisms to provide a head start on development of a diverse aquarium ecosystem.

Live Sand

Live sand is somewhat similar to live rock, in that it is harvested from the sea bottom and

A banded coral shrimp (**Stenopus hispidus**) *waits for its next meal.*

contains a natural population of beneficial small organisms. Whether it is essential to provide a plenum under several layers of substrate, as in the Jaubert-style system, is debatable. Simply placing a layer of coarse, dry sand on the bottom of the aquarium and allowing it to develop an infauna of bacteria, worms, and microcrustaceans appears to be all that is necessary for enhancing the microbial community of the mini-reef. The use of natural live sand as a source of "seed" organisms that will colonize a new sand bed is clearly beneficial. It seems clear from numerous reports in hobbyist magazines that incorporating a layer of substrate

into the mini-reef aquarium may speed up the establishment of a system that is in biological equilibrium (see "Troubleshooting," page 79). Ironically, in the past the use of substrate was discouraged by proponents of technically complex, overly "clean" mini-reef designs.

Wrasses offer a range of sizes and colors. This is a sixline wrasse (**Pseudocheilinus hexataenia**).

Summary

To develop a list of compatible species for a new marine tank, start by answering the following two questions:

- Do I want fish and invertebrates together?

    If the answer is "Yes," your fish selections must be "reef-compatible."
- Is there a fish or invertebrate that I absolutely must have?

    If the answer is "Yes," all other tank choices must revolve around this species.

Once you have made these choices, specifics will flow from your analysis of the characteristics of individual species. To help you I have provided two charts listing known compatibilities of marine fish and invertebrates. Please note that the rules are never absolute, and captive specimens may behave in unexpected ways. Nevertheless, these guidelines will help you avoid many common mistakes.

Marine Fish Compatibilities

Name	Compatible With	Incompatible With
Potter's Angelfish	Most sessile invertebrates	Males of its own species, and other Centropyge
Pygmy Angelfish	Most sessile invertebrates; may nip occasionally	Males of its own species, and other Centropyge
Bangaii Cardinalfish	Most reef-compatible fish and invertebrates	Shrimps small enough to swallow
Common Clownfish	Most reef-compatible fish and invertebrates	Other clownfish species
Maroon Clownfish	Most reef-compatible fish and invertebrates	Other clownfish species
Orange-Tailed Blue Damsel	Most invertebrates	Another male of its species, other damsels, sometimes other small fish
Tomato Clownfish	Most reef-compatible fish and invertebrates	Other clownfish species
Clark's Clownfish	Most reef-compatible fish and invertebrates	Other clownfish species
Neon Dottyback	Most invertebrates	Other dottybacks, unless a female mate
Orchid Dottyback	Most invertebrates, gets along with its own kind	Other dottybacks
Mandarin Dragonet	Most invertebrates	Large anemones or other stinging coelenterates; most other fish
Royal Gramma	Most invertebrates; gets along with its own kind	Dottybacks, other basslets
Blackcap Basslet	Most invertebrates	Other basslets, dottybacks
Rainford's Goby	Most invertebrates	Any aggressive species
Green-Striped Coral Goby	Most invertebrates	Any aggressive species
Neon Sharp-Nosed Goby	Most invertebrates	Any aggressive species
Limestriped Sharp-Nosed Goby	Most invertebrates	Any aggressive species

Citron Coral Goby	Most invertebrates	Any aggressive species
Long-Nosed Hawkfish	Most invertebrates	Shrimp small enough to swallow, other hawkfish
Flame Hawkfish	Most invertebrates	Other hawkfish
Yellow-Headed Jawfish	Most invertebrates	Most other fish; small shrimp
Hawaiian Turkeyfish	Its own kind	Anything edible
Hawaiian Lionfish	Its own kind	Anything edible
Swissguard Basslet	Most invertebrates	Other basslets
Sunburst Anthias	Most reef-compatible fish and invertebrates	Any aggressive species

Marine Invertebrate Compatibilities

Name	Compatible With	Incompatible With
Mushroom Polyp	Other mushroom polyps	Many corals
"Hairy" Blue Mushroom Polyp	Other mushroom polyps	Many corals
Leather Mushroom Soft Coral	Most fish	Negatively affects many other sessile invertebrates
Yellow Polyp Sea Mat	Most reef-compatible fish	May be stung by other sea mats
Green Star Polyp Soft Coral	Most reef-compatible fish	Aggressive, may encroach other sessile species
Pink-Tipped Anemone	Most invertebrates	May catch fish, stings other coelenterates
Bulb Anemone	Most crustaceans, larger fish	May catch fish other than clownfish
Curlicue Anemone	Most large fish	Can sting small fish, crustaceans, and other coelenterates
Open Brain Stony Coral	Most reef-compatible fish and invertebrates	May catch small fish, may be stung by soft corals
Giant Feather Duster	Most reef-compatible fish and invertebrates	Hermit crabs
Star Shell/Turban Shell	Most reef-compatible fish and invertebrates	Hermit crabs, wrasses, triggerfish
Giant Clams	Most reef-compatible fish and invertebrates	Most carnivorous organisms
Scarlet Cleaner and Peppermint Shrimp	Most reef-compatible fish and invertebrates	Can damage sessile invertebrates
Hermit Crabs	Most reef-compatible fish and invertebrates	May harm snails, worms
Banded Coral Shrimp	Most reef-compatible fish and invertebrates	Another banded coral shrimp
Curlicue Shrimp	Most reef-compatible fish and invertebrates	Can damage sessile invertebrates
Caribbean Slate Pencil Urchin	Non-aggressive fish	May feed on sessile invertebrates
Yellow Sea Cucumber	Most reef-compatible fish and invertebrates	Generally harmless, though toxic if eaten
Brittlestar and Serpent Star	Most reef-compatible fish and invertebrates	Harmless

SETTING UP A MINI-REEF MARINE AQUARIUM

In this chapter, I will take you through the process of setting up a mini-reef aquarium step by step. Although some readers may elect to follow this chapter as though it were a recipe, I urge you to use it as a starting point for creating a design that is uniquely your own. I have chosen to use a 30-gallon (113 L) tank for this example.

Why a 30-gallon (113 L) tank? It is large enough to accommodate a variety of organisms, and yet small enough to represent an affordable investment. Increasing the size of the aquarium increases the cost proportionately. The dimensions of a typical glass tank of 30-gallon capacity are 36 × 12 × 16 inches (91 × 30 × 40 cm) (L × W × H). In selecting a brand, remember that thicker glass and noticeably better workmanship denote quality and durability. The tank should come with a warranty against leakage. Settling upon a particular size tank simplifies choosing appropriate additional equipment.

Creating a Plan

Before buying anything, however, we need to create a plan for the aquarium and its

Reef tanks place the emphasis on colorful invertebrates with relatively few fishes.

inhabitants, as suggested in the chapter "Planning Your Aquarium." For purposes of this illustration, we will use two alternative plans. The first will be for a modest system without photosynthetic invertebrates, while the second will be for a more complex system and will include photosynthetic species. For the first system, we will choose as our model habitat an outer reef slope in the Caribbean. For the second, we will recreate a shallow lagoon area in Tonga.

Location, Location, Location

Give some thought to the location of the aquarium in the house, as site selection may have consequences for proper temperature maintenance. Remember that it is important for the tank temperature to remain stable, in the vicinity of 75°F (24°C). If the ambient temperature is close to this range, keeping the aquarium at the correct temperature is easy.

Temperature

Avoid locating the tank in front of a window. Although filtered sunlight, as is provided when the window is covered by a sheer drape or a translucent shade, is beneficial, temperature fluctuations near a window may be too great. Consider also the effects of ventilation. A stuffy room may get much warmer than a well-ventilated one. Similarly, if the tank is subjected to drafts, or is too close to a floor or wall vent, excessive heating and/or cooling of the water may occur. Take into account, also, the pattern of use the room receives. The kitchen or family room may routinely be warmer, for example, than a seldom-used spare bedroom. Of course, aquarists living in Georgia may have different temperature control problems than those living in North Dakota.

A simple way to tell if the aquarium will remain close to the desired temperature is to fill a new, well-rinsed 30-gallon (113 L) plastic trash can with tap water and place it in the approximate location of the planned aquarium. After 24 hours, check the temperature. If it is at 75°F (24°C) or less, perfect.

Heating the aquarium is easier, and much cheaper, than cooling it. For heating, you will need a submersible aquarium heater of about 100 watts. Heaters are usually reasonably priced. Cooling the water, on the other hand, requires a fluid chiller, which can be a costly piece of equipment. Selection and installation of a chiller is beyond the scope of this book. A constant temperature greater than 78°F (25°C) is detrimental to long-term success with a marine aquarium, despite the fact that many species may tolerate water temperature in excess of 80°F (27°C) for short periods. If your initial tests indicate that the place you have

chosen for the tank is too warm, you will have to decide either to install a chiller or to choose a cooler location. For the remainder of this chapter, we will assume that your aquarium can easily be maintained within a temperature range of 72 to 78°F (22–25°C).

Electrical Supply

An often-overlooked consideration regarding tank placement is the availability of an adequate electrical supply. You may need a multiple outlet strip to accommodate aquarium equipment. It is also wise to replace the outlet with a special Ground Fault Circuit Interrupter (GFCI) outlet. This device is recommended for wet locations, and is intended to reduce the shock hazard. Consult an electrician if necessary to ensure that the electrical supply to the aquarium is adequate and safe.

Support

Weight: Another point that deserves careful consideration is the nature of the support upon which the aquarium tank will rest. When filled, an aquarium weighs about 10 pounds (4.5 kg) per gallon of water capacity. Thus, the 30-gallon (113 L) tank in our example will weigh about 300 pounds (136 kg). If the support you choose is not designed for use as an aquarium stand, the importance of making sure it will not collapse under the weight of the tank is obvious. Less obvious, but equally important, is the need for a level support. If the tank is not absolutely level, water pressure will be unevenly exerted on the seams, increasing the likelihood of a leak. A weak, wobbly, uneven support is a recipe for disaster, with the potential for damage becoming greater as the size of the aquarium expands. (Aquariums above 60 gallons

(227 L) require additional support for the floor underneath, as well as a sturdy stand.)

Apart from the issue of sturdiness and level placement, the aquarium stand or cabinet is often designed to hide equipment, and to blend with the furniture in the room. Furniture design and craftsmanship is another subject beyond this book. Suffice it to say that a tank support sold along with the tank is probably your best choice, unless you are inclined to suffer the expense of having a tank stand custom built by a carpenter. Converting existing furniture for aquarium use is not recommended. Since the setup procedure is the same regardless of what type of support the tank is placed upon, I will assume, for the remainder of this chapter, that the tank will be sitting on a suitable support.

Backgrounds: Long experience in setting up aquariums has taught me that there are numerous little details that are best dealt with *before* the tank is filled with water. Chief among these is the installation of an opaque background. You can purchase backgrounds at the aquarium shop. These come in various materials and colors; there are even photographic reproductions of underwater scenes. If these appeal to you, by all means use them. I prefer a simple, solid color background of black or dark blue, however. While plastic film, foil, or cloth can be taped to the tank, a more permanent and satisfactory background is ordinary paint.

✔ Cover the areas where paint is unwanted with newspaper and masking tape, paying particular attention to sealing the interior of the tank against stray paint droplets.

✔ Thoroughly clean the glass to be painted with window cleaner, followed by wiping with a lint-free cloth moistened with rubbing alcohol.

The threadfin butterflyfish (Chaetodon auriga), *like many others of its family, will feed on delicate reef invertebrates.*

✔ Wait for the alcohol to evaporate completely, then simply apply at least two coats of exterior-grade spray enamel from the hardware store.

✔ Allow to dry according to the manufacturer's directions before proceeding with the aquarium setup.

✔ After removing the masking tape and paper, carefully clean the inside of the tank, using warm water with a small amount of vinegar. Rinse with clean water and dry thoroughly.

Basic Life Support System

The next step is to install the equipment that will provide lighting, water movement, and waste removal. If you have found that a heater is needed, it will also be installed at this point. Do not plug in any equipment until later.

• Place the aquarium on its support. Double-check to make sure the tank is level. Some hobbyists like to place a sheet of foam insulation

Dwarf lionfish (**Dendrochirus brachypterus**) *feed on crustaceans, mainly after darkness falls.*

board underneath the tank to help smooth out any imperfections in the surface and to aid in self-leveling as the foam collapses under the weight of the water.

• Install the heater at the rear of the tank, near the bottom, locating it so that the thermostat control is accessible for adjustment. Heaters are usually supplied with suction cups to facilitate installation.

• Install the protein skimmer according to the manufacturer's directions. A small skimmer designed to hang on the back of the tank is the best choice for our 30-gallon (113 L) beginner's system. Several good brands are available in aquarium shops. Although an internal skimmer will work just as well, I prefer to have as little equipment as possible visible inside the tank. You will find it most convenient to have the skimmer near one corner of the tank, to facilitate inspection and cleaning.

• Next, install at least one pump somewhere along the back wall of the tank with the outflow directed toward the front, to provide additional water circulation. The most widely available type of pump suitable for this application is the magnetic drive centrifugal pump known as a "powerhead" in the aquarium trade. For the system we are building, pumps that move about 200 gallons (757 L) per hour are a good choice.

Using two such pumps, controlled by an alternating timer known as a "wavemaker," is an even better idea, though not absolutely essential for success. Wavemakers allow the pumps to be switched on and off on a regular schedule, creating pulsed water movement that simulates ocean turbulence. This is essential for many invertebrates, and is beneficial for fish, providing them with appropriate exercise swimming against the current.

Lighting

For our initial, simplified mini-reef, lighting is not crucial. The single lamp fluorescent strip light fixture that is sold to accompany most brands of aquarium tanks is sufficient. One usually also has the option of purchasing either a plastic "hood" for the top of the tank, or a plate glass "canopy," along with the light fixture. Frequently, the tank, cover, and fixture are offered at a special combination price. I recommend the glass cover and separate strip light, especially if you plan to upgrade the tank later, because the lighting can be changed without installing a new cover. This is not an option with a plastic hood, which must be replaced should you wish to upgrade the lighting. Otherwise, lighting should pose few problems. Don't forget to buy a lamp. The usual fixture for our 30-gallon system accepts a lamp about 3 feet (91 cm) long that draws 30 watts of electricity. Much is often made about the different types of fluorescent lamps available. For this simple system, choose one that gives a pleasing visual effect (use your own judgment) and ignore the hype about the alleged benefits of one type versus another. Remember that one thing that makes this a "simplified" mini-reef is the absence of special lighting needs.

From a hardware store, purchase a timer to control the light fixture. Set the timer to provide 12 hours of lighting per day.

One important point about fluorescent light fixtures: choose one that will work with the timer. Some fixtures have a "preheat" requirement that will not permit this convenience.

The adult clown wrasse (**Coris gaimard**) *outdoes many other fish for sheer gaudiness.*

If in doubt, buy the timer first, and ask for a demonstration, before buying the fixture.

Equipment Check

Once the protein skimmer, water pumps, lighting, and (optional) heater are in place, it is wise to test them by filling the tank with tap water, plugging everything in, and allowing the equipment to run overnight.

Adjust the thermostat on the heater, if used, to the appropriate temperature at this time, also. Use an accurate thermometer to check the temperature of the water in the aquarium and make appropriate adjustments to reach the target temperature. You may need to readjust the heater several times to achieve the desired result. Several temperature checks over the next few hours will provide an indication of how well the heater is doing its job. The temperature should remain constant within a degree or two.

Adjust the water pump to direct a diagonal flow from the rear corner of the tank to the opposite front corner. If you are using two water pumps, direct them toward each other, so that the streams of water intersect. You may need to reposition them when live rock is added to the tank later.

The Protein Skimmer

The protein skimmer is a simple device that gets talked about a lot. The good brands come with instructions for installation and maintenance. Assuming that you have followed these instructions correctly, water should be circulating from the tank to the skimmer and back during the test. Little or no foam will be produced at this point, however, so final adjustments to the skimmer will have to be made later. This is why access to the skimmer is important. Now is the time to rearrange things, if necessary.

Stocking the Aquarium

If all goes well during this test, you are ready to proceed with the fun parts, building your miniature "reefscape" and stocking the aquarium with living organisms. First, disconnect the power to all equipment. Drain the tap water from the tank by siphoning it into a bucket with a length of hose. Fill the tank about two-thirds full with seawater prepared as described on page 70. (If you are the impatient type, you can make up 30 gallons (113 L) of seawater while you are running the equipment check.)

Adding the Sand Bed

Covering the bottom of the aquarium with an inch (2.5 cm) of sand, crushed coral, limestone gravel, aragonite, shell fragments, or (best of all) a mixture of these materials has been shown to improve the chemical stability of the system, in particular through enhanced denitrification, if used in a tank filled with live rock. Even if this were not the case, a layer of substrate looks more natural than placing the live rock directly on the glass tank bottom.

In a plastic bucket, rinse 50 pounds (23 kg) of substrate material, a portion at a time, in tap water until the water is only slightly cloudy. This step is important to remove fine, powdery material that accumulates in the sand bag during handling. Skipping this step does no harm, but it may take a while for the tank to clear. Give it at least a cursory rinse, as sometimes the product is contaminated with chips of wood or sea grass. You should end up with a layer of material about 1 inch (2.5 cm) deep on the tank bottom.

Both the appearance and biological activity of the substrate layer will be enhanced if a few pounds of live sand or live rock pebbles are added on top, with the live rock.

Adding the Live Rock

For our basic Caribbean system, I suggest using cultivated live rock from the Gulf or Mexico or the Florida Keys. You will need about 50 pounds (23 kg) of live rock to create a suitable reef structure in the 30-gallon (113 L) system. You may need to order live rock ahead of time, because of the curing process, so plan appropriately. It is imperative that the aquarium be filled with seawater and that all equipment is operating properly before introducing live rock. After adding the substrate, fill the tank to within about 1 inch (2.5 cm) of the top with prepared seawater. Reconnect all equipment and adjust it as needed. Just before adding the rock, you should remove some water and reserve it in a bucket, to allow for displacement. After all of the rock is in place, the tank can be topped off with the reserved seawater.

Placing the Rock

Unpacking the rock and placing it in the aquarium gives you an opportunity to be creative. Try to build a cave, since this will be a favorite haunt of the Royal Grammas that will, in this example, occupy the tank later. You can use plastic cable ties and/or underwater epoxy cement, both sold at aquarium shops and hardware stores, to hold rocks in position. Make sure the structure is stable. Place larger pieces near the bottom, and smaller ones on top, to avoid creating a top-heavy reef that may tumble down disastrously if someone slams a door nearby.

Start a few inches back from the front of the tank, and build a reef that slopes upward and back. Try to maintain an open structure through which water can easily move, rather than stacking the rocks like brickwork.

After all the rock has been placed, you can scatter live sand or live rock pebbles on the surface of the substrate, near the front of the tank. Double-check the temperature, specific gravity, and pH. Verify the timer settings on the light fixture. Adjust the wavemaker, if used.

You can stop here and pick up with the rest of the project as time permits, or you can proceed immediately with the next phase. From this point on, however, you are the custodian of a living ecosystem. Even though you cannot see the microorganisms on the live rock, they are already carrying out their vital biochemical tasks. It is important, therefore, to maintain the aquarium at optimum over the next several months, in order that these basic biological processes can be allowed to develop appropriately. This must be done regardless of the pace at which additional living organisms are added to the aquarium.

Stocking the Tank

For about six to eight weeks from the time you add live rock to the new aquarium, you can

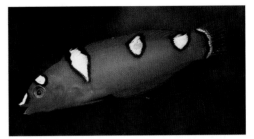

A juvenile clown wrasse (**Coris gaimard**) *looks nothing like an adult specimen.*

expect a series of algae blooms. Typically, brownish diatoms and reddish-purple cyanobacteria (also called "slime algae") are the first to make their appearance, followed by filamentous green algae. This is normal, and no special effort needs to be undertaken to eliminate them; trying to do so is futile, anyway. With the passage of additional time, assuming proper maintenance of the aquarium continues uninterrupted, the algae blooms will abate, and the first few patches of purple coralline algae will begin to appear on the glass or other solid surfaces. Coralline algae tend to grow best in moderate to dim light. Thus, new colonies often appear on the sides or back glass first. Eventually, several types of coralline algae will coat large areas of the glass and rocks. Use a razor blade to remove the algae from any area of the glass that you wish, but leave the other colonies undisturbed. The coralline algae is an important component of the mini-reef's ecosystem. Further, good coralline algae growth indicates that conditions in the aquarium are suitable for sessile invertebrates.

Algae Eaters

Because of the inevitable algae blooms early in the life of any aquarium, it is a good idea to choose for the first inhabitants of the aquarium an assortment of species that consume algae. Mollusks, such as the American Star Shell or Turban Snails, are widely available for this purpose. Other good choices include tiny Blue Leg Hermit Crabs, or the Scarlet Hermit Crab. You should have one individual crab or snail for each gallon of water in the aquarium, for effective long-term algae control.

Other "helper" species can also be added early in the aquarium's development. These include scavengers, such as assorted brittlestars, small shrimp such as the Peppermint Shrimp, and detritus feeding species such as certain sea cucumbers.

For the aquarium we are designing, add 30 of the algae-eaters about a week after you have added the live rock, or when the initial algae growth becomes noticeable. The following week add three Peppermint Shrimp and a brittlestar. Wait another week, and add another brittlestar, a Scarlet Cleaner Shrimp, and a detritus-feeding sea cucumber. Note that the recommended one-week interval between introductions of animals is somewhat arbitrary. You can wait a longer time, if you wish, or even put all of the specimens into the aquarium simultaneously. The latter approach, however, will not afford you an opportunity to correct problems early and avoid unnecessary losses of specimens if something is amiss. If the first introduction goes well and you are keeping up with routine maintenance, there should be few problems with future introductions.

The Main Attraction

After all of the algae-eating and scavenging invertebrate species have been added, the stage is set, as it were, for the main attraction. Three Royal Grammas will coexist peaceably in your mini-reef, if only one of them is male. To sex them, it is necessary to place a group of fish together and observe for typical male aggressive behavior. Two males face each other and gape, often so close that their snouts touch. This posturing apparently serves the same purpose as, for example, head-butting among bighorn sheep—males that are successful in the mock battle attract females for mating. Hopefully, your dealer will cooperate in helping you select a male Gramma. Choosing two females is easy: in a group of Grammas, the females ignore each other while the males go through their posturing routine. Incidentally, in the confines of the aquarium, where the "defeated" male has no opportunity to escape the notice of the "winner," the posturing may escalate into an actual battle, with one fish injuring the other. Thus, males must be separated from each other, once the sparring is over.

By now, the aquarium will be about two months old, and will have a thriving community of marine creatures. You can leave it at that, or you could add additional invertebrates, fanworms, for example, from the Florida Keys or Caribbean region. Once you have come this far successfully, you will no doubt develop other ideas on your own. I caution only against the temptation to add more fish. To do so will test the limits of the system's carrying capacity. Adding invertebrates, however, owing to the small demand they place on the system, is permissible.

A More Complex Design

If you are fascinated with invertebrates (and many hobbyists are) you may want to set up a more diverse mini-reef than the one just described. For this type of setup, the only significant difference from the previous example is the need for additional lighting. For invertebrates requiring a moderate light level, you must use two 30-watt fluorescent lamps. For shallow-water species accustomed to bright light, four such lamps will be needed. The example I have chosen, a shallow water lagoon habitat, therefore requires four lamps. Fixtures for aquariums are available that hold a pair of fluorescent lamps. You will need two of them, or you can purchase an aquarium lighting system designed to accommodate four lamps in a single fixture. In either case, use two timers to control each pair of lamps separately. You should adjust the timers so that one pair of lamps comes on about an hour before, and goes off about an hour after the other pair. This will simulate the increase and decrease in light levels at dawn and dusk.

Two powerheads controlled by a wavemaker should also be installed. In the simpler system previously under discussion, the second powerhead was optional. For this mini-reef, however, chaotic water movement is important. Currents bring food and oxygen to sessile invertebrates, and carry off wastes. It is better to err on the side of more water movement, rather than less.

Apart from these differences in equipment, the installation and setup of a lagoon tank is identical to the process just described. For this system, the Royal Gramma family will be replaced by three Orange-Tailed Blue Damselfish, one male and two females. Compared to the Royal Gramma, sexing this species is a simple matter: the male has an orange tail, and the female is all blue. Introduce all three fish at the same time, during the first two months after the live rock is added. Follow the instructions

above for adding algae-eaters and scavengers. When the system reaches equilibrium, and only then, photosynthetic invertebrates can be added as described below. Achievement of equilibrium occurs as algae blooms are replaced by coralline algae growth. (The much brighter lighting on this system may result in quite vigorous initial algae growth. Don't panic! The rampant growth will abate slowly, and in about two months the corallines will appear.) At equilibrium, as described in the next chapter, the concentration of nitrate in the water will fall to zero. This may take several months. If you are impatient, at least wait until nitrate is below 20 ppm before adding sessile, photosynthetic invertebrates.

The actual selection of invertebrates can be made from a variety of species that are collected in shallow water in the Indo-Pacific region. Good choices include Green Star Polyp Soft Coral, Leather Mushroom Soft Coral, and Disc Anemones. See "Fish and Invertebrates for the Beginner," page 43, for more detailed information. It makes no difference how many (within reason) of these species are included, nor does it matter in what order they are added. What is important is that the mini-reef ecosystem be sufficiently stable before these more demanding species are added. If you follow the instructions provided here, and in the chapter on maintaining the aquarium, everything should go smoothly. Once established, a system like this can thrive for many years with little additional attention, apart from weekly testing and adjustment of water conditions. One warning, however: I predict you will be considering an additional tank, or a larger tank, before the first year has elapsed. Mini-reef aquarium keeping can be habit-forming.

For some of the most routine adjustments, and for making artificial seawater, you will need, in addition to the chemical tests to be discussed shortly, an accurate hydrometer and an accurate thermometer. The hydrometer and thermometer measure specific gravity and temperature, respectively. Thermometers are no doubt familiar to everyone, so we will not dwell on the subject of temperature measurement, except to say that marine organisms do best at temperatures within the range of about 70 to 80°F (21–26°C), with the optimum being 75°F (24°C).

The hydrometer is used to measure specific gravity. Knowing the specific gravity allows one to estimate the

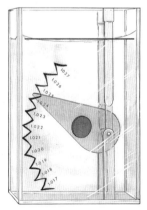

A simple hydrometer.

salinity of the water, if the temperature is known. "Salinity" refers to the amount of dissolved solids (salts) in the water. For the water bathing coral reefs, the salinity is 35 parts per thousand (ppt). For water of a given salinity, the specific gravity reading varies with the temperature. At 75° (24°C), the specific gravity of water at a salinity of 35 ppt is 1.0240. Follow the instructions for use that come with the hydrometer you select. Then use the information provided in Tables 4 and 5 to estimate the salinity of your aquarium from specific gravity readings.

Chemical Tests

Marine aquarists need to be able to perform the following tests:
✔ ammonia
✔ nitrite
✔ nitrate
✔ pH
✔ alkalinity
✔ calcium

Regardless of which brands of test kits you buy, follow the instructions for their use precisely. Always rinse out test vials thoroughly with fresh water after each use, then rinse the vial with the water to be tested prior to each use. Do not store test reagents for more than a year.

Nitrogen Compounds

Ammonia, nitrite, and nitrate are components of the biological filtration process. Proteins, found in every kind of food that might be eaten by a fish or an invertebrate, contain amino compounds. These eventually wind up in one of two places—in the proteins of the animal that consumed the food, or in the water, as excreted ammonia. As you might expect, fish and invertebrates do not thrive if forced to live in their own excreta. Fortunately, nitrifying bacteria can be cultivated in the aquarium. These bacteria convert ammonia first into nitrite and then into nitrate. Tests for ammonia and nitrite are used to determine if this process is proceeding correctly. Tests for each of these compounds should always be zero.

Nitrate, the end product of biological filtration, is tolerated by most marine organisms. However, the accumulation of waste compounds as the result of inadequate filtration or maintenance may be responsible for harmful effects, and such accumulation often parallels that of nitrate. Thus, measurement of nitrate can be used by the aquarist as a rough indicator of the overall condition of the system. It does little harm, in my view, to think of nitrate itself as undesirable, even though this is not strictly correct. The point is that the condition of aquarium water changes over time, that these changes are generally undesirable, and that they can be alleviated through maintenance. Nitrate is an easily measured indicator of the extent of these changes.

pH

The degree of acidity or alkalinity of the aquarium water is measured as pH. Seawater is alkaline, and has a pH of 8.3. In the aquarium, the minimum tolerable pH is about 7.8 or so. When an acid is added to seawater, the pH drops. Acid is a byproduct of the biological filtration process. In addition, when carbon dioxide is released into the water as a result of respiration by fish or invertebrates, it reacts with water to produce carbonic acid. Thus, the tendency in any aquarium is toward acidification, a decline in pH.

Photosynthetic organisms, such as algae growing in the aquarium, remove carbon dioxide from the water during the daytime and expel carbon dioxide into the water after darkness falls. This results in a daily fluctuation in pH, with the lowest point being just before the lights are turned on in the morning, and the highest point just before the lights go out in the evening. Measurements, therefore, should be made at a consistent time of day to facilitate appropriate comparisons.

Alkalinity

Alkalinity (which is also known as "buffer capacity," "KH," or "carbonate hardness") is a measure of the resistance of the water to a change in pH as acid is added. It is expressed in units called "milliequivalents per liter" (meq/L) and should be maintained at about 2.5 meq/L or above. If the alkalinity of the tank is at this

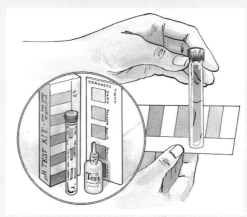

Testing the pH.

level or higher, it will be easier to maintain the correct pH. Allowing pH to fall too low can spell disaster for fish, which may suffer respiratory distress, and even death, as a result of the accumulation of carbon dioxide.

Maintaining the correct alkalinity is also important for invertebrates that secrete calcium carbonate shells or skeletal elements, such as mollusks and corals. For these organisms, it is essential that alkalinity be above 2.5 meq/L, that the pH be above 8.2, and that the calcium concentration of the water approximate that of natural seawater.

Calcium

Seawater contains about 400 ppm of calcium. Corals, soft corals, clams, snails, scallops, shrimp, crabs, starfish, sea urchins, and even some algae, extract calcium from the water continuously. Adding a calcium supplement, such as limewater, in amounts determined by testing the water for calcium on a regular basis, is important for these animals.

CARING FOR YOUR AQUARIUM

The waters bathing coral reefs are remarkable for their stability and for their very low concentrations of dissolved nutrients. Seawater confined in an aquarium, on the other hand, is subject to fluctuations and the accumulation of wastes.

The most important aspect of maintaining your marine aquarium is keeping certain parameters of the physical and chemical environment within rather narrow limits. This is easily accomplished by making regular observations and tests, and then carrying out appropriate adjustments. The aquarium's temperature can fluctuate with changing conditions in the room where the aquarium is kept, for example. Adjustments might thus involve something as simple as resetting a thermostat to keep the temperature of the aquarium constant despite room temperature fluctuations. Evaporation may cause a gradual, but significant, increase in salinity, as the same quantity of salts is concentrated in a smaller volume of water. Phosphate and other nutrient compounds can

Coral reef fish, such as this golden butterflyfish (Chaetodon semilarvatus) *sport brilliant coloration.*

accumulate to many times their natural levels, resulting in a bloom of algae growth. It is the aquarist's job to ensure that the magnitude of these inevitable changes in conditions is minimized through appropriate maintenance. Most of the time, this means testing the water regularly and making appropriate adjustments when conditions begin to deviate from their target values. "Test, then tweak" is the rule of thumb. Neglecting maintenance can necessitate a massive water change.

Making Seawater

Some hobbyists find that changing some water on a regular basis is the best way to maintain the aquarium in good shape. Others change water only when tests indicate that too many nutrients are accumulating. Some never change water, except perhaps in an emergency. Regardless of the approach you ultimately

Scott's fairy wrasse (**Cirrhilabrus scottorum**) *and a banana wrasse* (**Halichoeres chrysus**) *illustrate the wide range of coloration in the wrasse family.*

choose as the best one for your aquarium, sooner or later you will need to replace some seawater. Thus, making and storing synthetic seawater is a basic skill.

It is worth noting that aquarists who have convenient access to natural seawater should use it whenever possible. Some hobbyists elect to disinfect freshly collected seawater by adding chlorine, allowing the water to sit overnight, and then removing the chlorine with a commercial dechlorinator. Others simply allow the water to stand, covered, in a cool, dark place for a week or so. In some large coastal cities, seawater can be purchased from service companies who collect, disinfect, and deliver the water to your door. For the majority of hobbyists, however, synthetic seawater, made up using dry salt mix and fresh water, is the most satisfactory way to obtain this essential component of any marine aquarium.

Regardless of the source, replacement seawater must be similar to the water in the tank in terms of its temperature, specific gravity, and pH before you add it to an established aquarium.

If stored covered in a cool, dark place such as a garage, basement, or closet, seawater keeps indefinitely, so it is easy to mix up a large amount to have available for water changes as needed. Choose a container suitable for food for storing seawater. A covered plastic container is ideal.

Strangely, aquarists do not often give thought to the quality of the freshwater that they use to prepare synthetic seawater, and most use plain tap water. I would recommend strongly against this, as, unfortunately, municipal tap water and well water are frequently unsatisfactory for aquarium use. This is due to the presence of pollutants that, while perhaps not deemed harmful for drinking purposes, can cause problems in the marine aquarium. Algae nutrients such as phosphate and silica, toxic metals such as copper, and a host of other compounds may all be found in "pure" tap water. I recommend that all water used for the marine aquarium be purified in some way.

The RO System

For hobbyists with minimal water requirements, the best bet may be simply to purchase distilled water. For any significant amount of purified water, however, it is much cheaper in the long run to purify tap water at home using a reverse osmosis (RO) system. This technique uses water pressure to force tap water through a special membrane, in effect "straining out" pollutants. RO units produce, on average, water that is about 90 percent free of contaminants. RO units have two drawbacks: Water is produced drop by drop, with typical units producing 15 to 25 gallons (57–94 L) of water per day, so a reservoir is needed. Also, about 4 gallons (15 L) of waste water are produced for every gallon of product water. The waste water can be used for laundry or irrigation purposes.

If the tap water bears an unusually heavy load of contaminants, some troublesome compounds, such as phosphate, for example, may remain in the product water in an amount sufficient to cause problems in the aquarium. If this turns out to be the case in your community, RO water may need further purification by the use of deionization. This technique employs chemical resins to absorb undesirable substances from the water. The addition of a deionization filter to an RO system can provide water comparable to glass-distilled water. Deionization can also be used as the sole means of water purification, dispensing with RO altogether, but this is a more expensive option, as the special resins must be periodically replaced, and they are costly. The advantages of using deionization alone are that water is produced on demand, not dropwise, and there is no waste-water production. Always use distilled, deionized or RO water for making synthetic seawater.

Stored Seawater

A little more than two cups of dry seawater mix will make 5 gallons (19 L) of seawater. Buy dry salt mix in large quantities to save on its cost. It keeps indefinitely if stored in a tightly sealed container away from moisture, which promotes caking.

A common problem with stored seawater is that the storage temperature is cooler than the temperature of the tank. Here are two tips for solving this problem.

1. Make a concentrated brine by dissolving the required amount of salt in only two-thirds as much water as you are going to need. When ready to use, add heated fresh water to the brine to dilute it to the correct specific gravity.

2. Alternatively, prepare water to the desired specific gravity and store it. When ready to use, heat a portion of the water to the temperature of a cup of coffee using your microwave oven, and mix the heated water back into the cooler water to raise its temperature to that of the tank.

Note: Never heat seawater to the boiling point, and never heat it in a metal container.

Feeding

Of all the factors that occupy the interest of aquarists in the course of caring for their tanks, perhaps none is given less attention than the quality of the diet of the animals. In a well-established mini-reef, there will be an abundance of small organisms, microcrustaceans, and algae, for example, that serve as food for filter-feeding invertebrates and fish. While these foods are perhaps the best kind of nourishment for captive specimens, they cannot be relied upon to support a reasonably large fish population indefinitely. In other words, the fish will need to be fed, perhaps infrequently, in any marine aquarium. The quantity of food given is important, but equally important is its nutritional quality.

Feeding Schedule

Never mind that the fish always seem hungry when you approach the tank. The fact that they are willing to eat does not mean that they should be fed. Establish a regular feeding schedule and stick to it.

Added Foods

Added foods are a major source of nutrient ions, and the concentration of these substances in the water must be kept to a minimum. A large proportion of these nutrient ions will find their way into the water whether eaten or not. Nevertheless, the food supply should be adjusted so that the fish consume as much of the food as possible and little sinks to the bottom to decay. Deciding how much to give at a feeding will take some experimentation on the part of the aquarist, as each community of fish is different.

Feed as wide a variety of foods as possible. Fish need a balanced diet for all of the same reasons that you do. Fresh, living foods are preferable to any sort of prepared foods. However, convenience will dictate that prepared foods will have to be used at least part of the time. It is also important that the diet come from marine organisms, as opposed to terrestrial or freshwater species, whenever possible.

Live Foods

Adult brine shrimp, newly hatched brine shrimp, amphipods, California blackworms, guppies, and baitfish are commonly available. Any of these live foods may be given to fish that will eat them, which includes most aquarium species. Do not make the mistake, however, of feeding marine fish exclusively on blackworms, guppies, or baitfish.

Fresh Foods

Few aquarium shops stock fresh foods, because of the short shelf life of these products. However, your grocery stocks an abundance of foods that can be used in the aquarium. Fresh fish fillets, shrimp, clams, scallops, mussels, and squid can be chopped into pieces of a size appropriate for feeding aquarium fish. Ocean fish, such as snapper, tuna, mahi-mahi, halibut, sole, cod, and grouper, are better choices than freshwater fish, such as trout and catfish. The produce department stocks a host of vegetables that are good for herbivorous marine fish. Lettuce, spinach, parsley, peas, broccoli, and zucchini have all been used with success. If the fish are finicky about eating these foods initially, blanch them briefly in boiling water before feeding. This will make their consistency more like that of the algae that herbivorous fish are accustomed to eating. Use foods from terrestrial sources sparingly, as a supplement to, and not as a replacement for, ocean-derived foods.

Frozen Foods

Frozen foods sold for aquarium use range from individual organisms, such as brine shrimp, squid, mysid shrimp, or lancefish, to complex preparations containing a variety of ingredients and additives. One manufacturer even makes a food containing sponges, an important constituent in the diet of some marine angelfish. Manufacturers often supply the foods in cube packs, which is very convenient. Frozen foods

Tables 4 and 5
Estimating Salinity from Specific Gravity

When the specific gravity of aquarium water is measured with a hydrometer, the salinity of the water can be calculated if the temperature is also known.

First, convert the temperature reading to Celsius, by using the following formula:

°C = 0.56 (°F − 32)

Next, read across to find the temperature in Table 5, and then read down in that column to the row corresponding to the hydrometer reading. The number in the table is a conversion factor, which should be added to the hydrometer reading. The result is the density of the water.

Finally, using Table 6, look up the salinity that corresponds to the density you just calculated.

Table 4: Conversion of Specific Gravity Readings to Density

Specific gravity	Temperature (°C)						
	20°	21°	22°	23°	24°	25°	26°
1.0170	10	12	15	17	20	22	25
1.0180	10	12	15	17	20	23	25
1.0190	10	12	15	18	20	23	26
1.0200	10	13	15	18	20	23	26
1.0210	10	13	15	18	21	23	26
1.0220	11	13	15	18	21	23	26
1.0230	11	13	16	18	21	24	26
1.0240	11	13	16	18	21	24	27
1.0250	11	13	16	18	21	24	27
1.0260	11	13	16	19	22	24	27
1.0270	11	14	16	19	22	24	27
1.0280	11	14	16	19	22	25	28
1.0290	11	14	16	19	22		

Table 5: Conversion of Density to Salinity

Density	Salinity	Density	Salinity	Density	Salinity
1.0180	25	1.0225	30	1.0270	36
1.0185	25	1.0230	31	1.0275	37
1.0190	26	1.0235	32	1.0280	38
1.0195	27	1.0240	32	1.0285	38
1.0200	27	1.0245	33	1.0290	39
1.0205	28	1.0250	34	1.0295	40
1.0210	29	1.0255	34	1.0300	40
1.0215	29	1.0260	35		
1.0220	30	1.0265	36		

Natural salinity is 35 in the vicinity of most coral reefs, unless the ocean is diluted from a nearby freshwater source. The acceptable range for invertebrates is 34 to 36, while fish can tolerate lower salinities.

Water Quality Parameters for Mini-Reef Aquariums

Temperature	75°F (optimum)
	72–78°F (acceptable)
Specific Gravity	1.022–1.0240
pH	8.15–8.6
	(8.2–8.3 optimum)
Alkalinity	2.0–5.0 meq/L
Ammonia (NH_3)	Zero
Nitrite (NO_2^-)	Zero
Nitrate (NO_3^-)	<20 mg/L (ion)
Phosphate (PO_4^{-3})	<0.05 mg/L
Calcium (Ca^{+2})	375–475 mg/L
Dissolved Oxygen (O_2)	>6.90 mg/L

are probably the best substitute for fresh foods, and come in a much wider variety. Of course, frozen foods are always available, whereas fresh or live foods may not be. Keep a variety of frozen foods on hand and feed them to your fish regularly. After thawing, frozen foods may be fed in quantities comparable to live and fresh food feedings.

Freeze-dried Foods

Freeze drying preserves almost as much nutritional value as freezing, although certain vitamins are lost in the process. Most freeze-dried aquarium foods contain crustaceans, such as krill or brine shrimp. These foods are nutritionally concentrated and are convenient, but should not form the staple diet for marine fish, as they are mostly protein, lacking a broader range of nutrients. Freeze-dried brine shrimp,

for example, has not been shown to be a complete dietary substitute for living brine shrimp. Use freeze-dried foods as a supplement to other foods, to provide variety.

Dehydrated Flake Foods

Dehydrated flake foods are cheap and convenient, and certain to be stocked by any aquarium shop. Choose flake foods that are specifically blended to meet the nutritional requirements of marine fish. Dried seaweed is a suitable alternative to the fresh product. Vegetarian fish love it, and it is a more natural food for them than garden vegetables.

Despite the cost savings that accrue when flake foods are bought in quantity, it is best to purchase only a small amount at any one time. After opening, flake foods may lose food value, or worse, develop mold or bacterial growth.

Handling Aquarium Foods

Frozen foods for the aquarium should be treated like frozen foods for human consumption. Keep frozen, thaw out only what you need, and do not refreeze completely thawed food. All foods should be purchased in small quantities that will be used within a reasonable period of time (one month, or less), and should be stored in the freezer or refrigerator to facilitate maximum retention of nutritional value. Keep all foods tightly sealed, as oxygen from the air can break down valuable vitamins, and moisture intrusion can lead to spoilage.

Many aquarists are concerned about transmitting disease to their fish via fresh or frozen seafoods. This is unlikely. Often in nature sick or injured fish are eaten by other fish with no ill effects. Disease outbreaks in the aquarium can usually be traced to less than optimal water

The sunburst anthias (**Serranocirrhitus latus**) *will eat a variety of small food items.*

quality, or other conditions that create stress for the fish and leave them more susceptible to infection. Feeding a wholesome, balanced diet is one way to prevent disease outbreaks.

A proper feeding regimen for your mini-reef is easy to establish. First, learn all you can about the natural diet of the fish you intend to keep, and try to duplicate this as closely as possible in the aquarium. Second, feed as wide a variety of foods as possible. Third, experiment. Try different brands and types of foods available from your dealer. Each time you purchase fish food, buy one that you have not used recently. Also experiment with fresh seafoods and greens from the grocery store. Providing a nutritious, varied diet is one of the easiest and least costly aspects of maintaining a marine tank. Feed your fish once or twice daily, less often if the tank has an abundant growth of microinvertebrates and algae. While some species are specialized in their dietary require-

ments, the majority of coral reef fish eat a variety of foods. On the reef, of course, all the foods are fresh, and algae, sponges, shrimp, and coral polyps are always on the menu.

Record Keeping

Record the following information about each aquarium in a log book. Having written records makes spotting trends a cinch. Often, problems can thus be detected and corrected in time to avoid serious consequences.

✔ date
✔ test(s) performed and results
✔ anything added and amount
✔ temperature
✔ specific gravity and calculated salinity
✔ amount of water changed
✔ species and size of fish or other animals added
✔ incidents of death or disease, treatments, and results
✔ any comments or pertinent observations

Regular testing, good records, and consistent maintenance are the keys to success.

Summary

I have summarized basic water quality parameters in the table on page 74. The numbers I have supplied are based on experience as well as extensive reading and discussions with many aquarists. To make sure you maintain the water chemistry of your marine aquarium within appropriate limits, you should purchase good test kits, use them on a regular basis, and keep a written record of the results.

How often is "a regular basis"? I suggest keeping a daily record of temperature, specific

With proper aquarium care, this pair of Tomato Clownfish (**Amphiprion frenatus**) *may even produce offspring.*

gravity, and pH readings. Make these observations at a specific time of day, right after you have dinner, for example. You should note little deviation from one day to the next. A sudden large change in any of these three key parameters is cause for concern. Investigate further to determine the cause. Has a heater stopped working? Is a pump unplugged?

Measure alkalinity and nitrate on a weekly basis. Changes in alkalinity and nitrate typically occur at a slower pace than changes in temperature or pH. You may find that you need to add an alkalinity booster to increase the reading, or that enough nitrate has accumulated to necessitate a partial water change. Expect alkalinity to decline, and nitrate to increase, over the course of a week. You will quickly learn, if you keep accurate notes, the trend for your particular aquarium system. Once that trend has been established, a significant deviation should signal potential trouble with the system.

Ammonia and nitrate tests should only be performed when you suspect a problem. Fish and invertebrates may exhibit signs of stress, or develop a disease condition as a result of the invisible accumulation of one or both of these compounds. When this occurs, it signals that the key water management process taking place in the tank, biological filtration, is failing. This situation is the equivalent of a boat taking on water. At first, the threat may not appear severe, but with time, the situation becomes dire. If you find either ammonia or nitrite present in your aquarium, take immediate corrective action. Check to make sure the biological filter is operating properly. Find and remove anything that might be decomposing, such as a dead animal or piece of uneaten food. If you are unsure, carry out a 30 percent water change. This can buy time to root out the cause of the problem, and will not further harm the tank.

Juvenile angelfish, such as this Blue Ring Angel (**Pomacanthus annularis**) *will mature to spectacular adults in a roomy, well-maintained tank.*

Although necessary, good water quality is not sufficient for success. Fish will suffer stress and develop problems if they do not receive proper nourishment, if they fight, or if the aquarium is too crowded to satisfy their needs for swimming space. For this reason, you should keep track of your aquarium observations as often as possible. If you notice a squabble, for example, determine its severity. Minor territorial skirmishes often subside on their own, with no damage to either contender. Continual harassment, however, will often result in the victim's developing a parasite infestation or other stress-induced problems that can spread to the rest of the tank. Observe the tank carefully over the next few days to make sure all is well.

Being alert for potential problems is a good thing. Taking prompt action when trouble looms is a good thing. But try to avoid constantly making changes and "fiddling" with the aquarium setup. Starting out with a plan will go a long way toward avoiding mistakes that demand major changes. Try to keep minor adjustments to a minimum, as well. The old adage, "If it ain't broke, don't fix it," strongly applies to marine aquariums.

Acquiring a "salty thumb" is not automatic with the purchase of an aquarium tank. Successful marine aquarists develop the ability to recognize potential problems before they become catastrophes. Be patient. Assume you will make mistakes early in the game, and resist the temptation to purchase rare and/or demanding species until you have gained experience with fish and invertebrates known to be well-adapted to life in captivity.

TROUBLESHOOTING

Marine invertebrates and fish are surprisingly free from acute bacterial infections or infestations of parasites when not exposed to stress-producing factors.

An Ounce of Prevention

Again and again, experience teaches us that maintaining the correct environmental parameters, providing a proper diet, and protecting captive marine organisms from physical damage are ultimately simpler and more effective than attempting to control a disease or parasite outbreak once begun.

Experience also teaches that sometimes, unavoidably, the hobbyist will be faced with the necessity of treating a fish that has developed an infestation of parasites. I have therefore included instructions for applying an effective remedy.

Common Problems and Solutions

Parasites

It is worth repeating that the key to avoiding an infestation of parasites, perhaps the

This Lemon Peel Angelfish (Centropyge flavissimuss) shows all the signs of good health: erect fins, bright coloration, and alertness.

most commonplace problem facing marine aquarists, is to provide conditions that promote good health in the fish population. In the ocean, the fish's immune system largely protects it from infestations of *Cryptocaryon* (white spot) and *Amyloodinium* (coral fish disease). Maintaining good health in the fish involves practicing good aquarium management. When you bring a new specimen home from the dealer, place it in a separate tank for a couple of weeks to observe its behavior. This will prevent any problem that may develop in the new fish from spreading to other, established specimens. In addition, isolating new specimens in a separate tank makes the job of treating them much easier, if a need for treatment does develop.

Treatment: Should treatment for white spot or coral fish disease become necessary, the only truly effective medication is copper. Use an ionic (not "chelated") copper medication, and use a copper test kit to determine when the correct dosage has been added to the treatment tank. A copper concentration of 0.15–0.20 ppm is most effective. Below 0.15 ppm, the treatment will not be effective; above 0.20 ppm, the copper is stressful to the fish. These values are suggested

TIP

Copper Medications

Copper medications should never be used in a tank containing invertebrates, as most invertebrates are rapidly killed by therapeutic levels of copper. This is another good reason to have a separate treatment tank.

by a manufacturer of copper test kits and a copper treatment for marine aquariums, as well as by my personal observations. Spotte (1992) points out that higher copper concentrations may be more effective. However, he also notes that the effects of copper on marine fish can be detrimental. Marine fish should never be routinely dosed with copper as a preventive measure, for this reason.

Symptoms: Symptoms are similar for both *Cryptocaryon* and *Amyloodinium*, and include rapid shallow breathing, scratching, hiding, poor appetite, loss of color, and the appearance of small white dots on the fish's body and fins. These parasite problems commonly appear in fish that have recently been transported from the point of capture, and in tanks that have experienced some sudden departure from good water conditions. When a fish is under stress, it is more likely to succumb to a parasite infestation.

Amyloodinium, the more deadly of the two parasites, produces a substance, apparently not unlike that involved in "red tides," that is toxic to fish. This is in addition to the *Amyloodinium* organism's penchant for feeding upon and destroying the fish's gills, causing death by

oxygen starvation if left untreated. Beginners may not be able to diagnose *Amyloodinium* until it is too late to save the infected fish, because by the time external symptoms appear, the damage to the gills has already been done. My advice to beginners is simple: If any fish appears to be breathing at a more rapid rate than the others, or more rapidly than you are accustomed to seeing as a "normal" breathing rate, treat the entire fish population promptly with copper. When a fish's gills are damaged by a parasite infestation, the fish breathes more rapidly to compensate, and normal breathing does not resume until the infestation is alleviated.

Excessive Algae

Tangs, angelfish, some blennies, and many kinds of snails all benefit from being able to graze on algae growth in the tank. Algae becomes a problem only when it interferes with the aesthetic appeal of the tank, or when rampant growth threatens to smother delicate organisms such as sessile invertebrates. Unfortunately, there is no simple approach to controlling excess algae growth, because a variety of factors are involved in its development. Of primary importance is the accumulation of excessive levels of nutrient ions in the aquarium. These substances are in relatively short supply in the natural environment of the coral reef. In the aquarium, however, they can rapidly accumulate, providing "fertilizer" for explosive growths of filamentous, encrusting, and free-floating algae species.

Phosphate

Phosphate seems to be the nutrient most often implicated in the appearance of an algae bloom. Phosphate is ubiquitous in nature, and finds its way into the aquarium from a variety of sources. These include all foods, some salt mixes and tank additives, and especially tap water. In every case that I have had the opportunity to investigate, a tank overgrown with algae also contains a high concentration of phosphate. Removal of accumulated detritus on a regular basis will help to eliminate phosphates. If your salt mix contains phosphates, switch to a brand that does not. You can evaluate your current brand easily by performing a phosphate test on a freshly mixed batch of water. You should perform a phosphate test on a sample of your tap water, also. If the tap water contains phosphates, you will have to decide if your algae problem is sufficiently severe to warrant purifying the tap water before use, by means of reverse osmosis, deionization, or some other means. If your water requirements are small, you can purchase distilled water at the grocery store.

Lighting

Lighting also plays a role in algae growth. For example, in tanks that formerly grew little algae, the appearance of a bloom may indicate the need to change fluorescent or metal halide lamps. As lamps age, their intensity diminishes and their spectral output changes, and this may trigger a growth of undesirable algae where none was previously present.

Unidentified Organisms

After an aquarium has been established, tiny crustaceans and worms sometimes appear. These hitchhike into the tank with fish and invertebrate specimens, and feed on organic matter and algae. The commonly observed

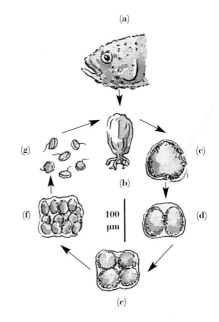

Life cycle of Amyloodinium.
a) Trophonts on infected fish
b) Trophont (enlarged)
c–f) Tomonts
g) Dinospore (resting stage)

species are capable of reproduction in the aquarium, and sometimes multiply to high population densities.

Several organisms are in this category. Amphipods are shrimplike crustaceans about 1/4 inch (6 mm) in length. Copepods, another crustacean, are only about 1/16 inch (1.6 mm) in length, appearing as white specks moving around on the glass and rocks. Flatworms are about 1/8 inch (3 mm) long, with a rounded head end and forked tail in the most commonly seen species. They are translucent, and are usually seen gliding on the glass. Nematodes are short, white, threadlike worms usually less than

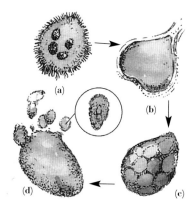

Life cycle of Cryptocaryon.
a) Trophont—parasitic stage
b) Tomont—reproductive stage
c) Tomont with developing tomites
d) Tomite—infective stage

$1/4$ inch in length. All of these are harmless scavengers, but the presence of any of them in great abundance indicates that excessive detritus is accumulating, or that uneaten food or a dead animal is decomposing unnoticed. Removal of any deteriorating organic matter, and siphoning detritus from the tank will lower the numbers of these organisms.

Power Failure

In a well-maintained mini-reef that is not overcrowded, a power outage of a few hours is not usually cause for concern. If the outage extends beyond about four hours, you can take the following precautions:

✔ Cover the tank with a heavy quilt or blanket to retard heat loss.

✔ Every half hour, dip some water out of the tank with a clean pitcher and pour it back in from a height of about one foot, to aerate the water.

✔ As soon as power is restored, check to make sure all equipment has restarted properly, and plan to do a partial water change the following day.

✔ If the outage has lasted longer than eight hours, test the tank for ammonia, nitrite, pH, and alkalinity, and observe the inhabitants carefully for problems that may develop over the next several days. If a week goes by without noticeable trouble, you can rest easy.

If you live in an area that is subject to frequent power outages of long duration, you might want to consider a battery operated air pump as a backup. If your aquarium is large, or your fish collection is an unusually valuable one, an emergency generator may be a prudent investment.

Nutrition-related Problems

Head and lateral line erosion (HLLE) is characterized by erosion of the skin tissue along the lateral line and around the face. It occurs especially in tangs and angelfish. HLLE results from vitamin deficiency. Prevention and cure simply involves feeding fish fresh foods that are high in vitamins A and C, or the less desirable approach of adding supplements that contain these vitamins to frozen and dried foods. Some vitamins are difficult to preserve, hence the need for fresh foods and/or supplements.

A different form of malnutrition can affect large, predatory fish such as lionfish. Feeding lionfish exclusively on freshwater baitfish, once a common practice, condemns the lionfish to an early death from thiamine deficiency. To avoid the problem, feed ocean-derived foods, not those from terrestrial or freshwater sources.

Porcupine fish and spiny boxfish can lose the ability to move their jaws, and may lose all their teeth, as well, if fed freeze-dried krill (*Euphausia pacifica*) exclusively for several months. In nature, fish such as these feed on a wide variety of invertebrates and smaller fish. It is not surprising that they would suffer problems from a diet consisting of a single food. The fish eventually die of starvation, or become so debilitated that they must be euthanized.

Avoiding nutritional problems in marine fish is easy if you follow my advice. Feed marine fish the widest possible variety of foods, and choose only foods derived from marine sources wherever possible.

Plankton Substitutes

Supplying an appropriate diet for invertebrates (and some fish) that feed on the tiny organisms collectively known as "plankton" can prove challenging. If you are unable or unwilling to give the extra effort needed to supply a plankton substitute, you should avoid these organisms altogether. Fortunately, convenience foods exist for even these finicky creatures, but you should not rely solely on prepared diets. Living algae cultures offer one option. They usually contain one or more unicellular marine algae and have a reasonably long shelf life.

Brine shrimp: For species, such as many corals, that will eat somewhat larger prey, it is hard to beat newly hatched brine shrimp (*Artemia*). The resting cysts, often incorrectly called "eggs," store nearly indefinitely. Most shops stock them. To hatch, fill a quart jar with water and add three tablespoons of synthetic seawater mix. Place the jar in a brightly lit area, but away from direct sun. Bubble air through the water using a small air pump and air diffuser from the aquarium shop. Add a large pinch of the brownish colored cysts. In about 48 hours, the cysts will hatch, and you will see the tiny shrimp swimming around jerkily. The water surface will bear a floating raft of empty and unhatched cysts. Avoid putting them into your aquarium. Shine a flashlight at a spot on one side of the jar, several inches from the top. This will attract the shrimp, which can be removed with a medicine dropper or small, fine-meshed net, leaving the cysts behind. Try to feed all the hatched shrimp within two days, as they rapidly lose their nutritional value if they are not themselves fed on algae.

Lower tank: Another approach taken by some aquarists requires setting up a separate, small aquarium tank below the main tank and circulating water from the main tank through the lower tank. The lower tank thus becomes a "refugium" for small organisms that naturally reproduce in the aquarium. The refugium allows their numbers to increase in the absence of the hungry mouths waiting in the display tank. After the refugium has been set up for a month or two, it will be teeming with helpful, barely visible critters of many kinds. You can harvest any time and feed the main tank.

One final note: The longer an aquarium has been established, the more likely it is to develop a natural population of beneficial microorganisms and tiny invertebrates. It takes a year or more for an aquarium to mature. Be patient. You will have much better luck if you wait a while before adding the more demanding kinds of organisms to the tank.

Aggression

It's a harsh world, and the coral reef is no exception. Eat or be eaten is the rule; danger and disaster lurk in every crevice and behind every head of coral. It should come as no sur-

Male wrasses, such as this Laboute's Fairy Wrasse (**Cirrhilabrus laboutei**) *show aggression only toward other males.*

prise, therefore, that aggression between two tank mates can be a significant problem for an aquarium with a mixed community of fish and/or invertebrate species. Even seemingly harmless, sessile corals may be locked in mortal combat with their equally meek-appearing neighbors. Since you choose the species that go into your captive reef, you can keep such problems to a minimum by making wise selections.

Beyond the obvious strategy of not placing a predator in the same tank with its prey, keep in mind a few rules of thumb when shopping for fish. A given reef fish is most likely to show aggression toward a member of its own species. Unless you know for certain they will get along, do not place multiple individuals of the same species in the same tank.

Where there are significant differences in appearance between the sexes, the larger or more brightly colored individual is usually the more aggressive. Often, but not always, this is the male. As a rule, the male of a species will tolerate a female in the same tank, perhaps even several females, but not another male.

The bright coloration for which reef fish are so valued by aquarists, permits one fish to readily identify another in a chance encounter. As a result, if a given species shows aggression toward members of its own species, it will likely react with aggression toward a different species that is similarly colored. This behavior is intensified if the offender is also similar to the aggressor in shape and size. It makes sense, therefore, to avoid placing fish of closely similar appearance in the same tank.

The size of a fish's territory is strongly influenced by its lifestyle. Far-ranging species, such as tangs, may consider the entire aquarium their domain, and no other tang will be permitted to enter. Fish that stay in one spot, such as clownfish, may be tethered within their "safety zone" and seldom stray. In this situation, only fish that enter the zone will be attacked.

Some fish are simply more aggressive by nature. Damselfishes are widely recognized as fearless and willing to attack fish much larger than themselves. At the other end of the spectrum are retiring types like the jawfishes, who prefer to hide rather than attack an intruder. You are sorely tempting fate if you try to keep both types together. Aggressive species are best housed with equally robust tank mates. The meek should be permitted a tank to themselves.

Aggression among corals is more subtle. Some simply outgrow their neighbors to win the struggle for available space. Others can fatally sting species that grow too close. Still others can release toxic compounds into the water to make the surroundings unwelcoming to potential competitors. The only way to determine with certainty who will live with whom is to experiment. Fortunately, over the years, hobbyists and professionals alike have noted which corals are a danger to their tank mates and which ones are not. Patterns emerge. For example, many popular soft corals can severely sting other corals placed too close. Mushroom corals, also known as false corals, can sting, too. These are known as aggressive corals. On the other hand, some popular hard corals typically wind up the losers in any sting-ing contest, and are considered nonaggressive.

Toxicity

Numerous reef denizens, in order to avoid becoming dinner for a hungry predator, have evolved toxic flesh. If eaten, such species often kill the diner. From the perspective of the prey, however, it does little good to kill the predator if you are eaten. As a result, toxic species usu-ally evolve warning coloration. Because warning coloration can be bold and arresting, toxic species may enjoy considerable popularity. Sea apples, of which there are several species, pro-vide a good example of invertebrate toxicity and warning coloration. Sea apples are marked in primary colors, bright reds, electric blues, and fluorescent yellows. If one of these specimens dies in the aquarium, its toxicity can kill every fish in the tank.

Similarly, scientists believe the mandarin dragonet wears a psychedelic color pattern to announce to other fish that it should be avoided as prey. Hobbyists have reported the death of large predators, such as lionfish, after consuming a mandarin. Further, it does appear that aquarium fish generally leave them alone.

Understanding some basic biological facts about the fish and invertebrates you place in your marine tank will help you avoid needless losses. Always ask for this type of information whenever you make a purchase. Better still, research potential purchases before you make them and arrive at the fish store with a plan in mind.

Juvenile fish may be more sensitive to toxic conditions than their adult counterparts. This is a juvenile Emperor Angelfish (**Pomecanthus imperator**).

HOW-TO: TWEAK

Nitrogen Compounds

If biological filtration is proceeding normally, there should never be a trace of ammonia or nitrite in the water. Finding either during a routine test is cause for concern. Typical causes are: too many fish; uneaten food or decay of a dead animal; an antibiotic has been added, killing the nitrifying bacteria (often done in an attempt to treat some other problem); or a shortage of oxygen (often the result of pump failure, or because the tank becomes too warm). Appropriate corrective action might involve removing some fish, siphoning out decaying matter, removing the antibiotic with activated carbon filtration or by doing a large water change, fixing the pump, or taking steps to lower the temperature. Fish exposed to ammonia and nitrite often subsequently develop parasite infestations, which must be dealt with appropriately.

Overloading

The main reason for admonishments against overfeeding is the need to minimize the input to the nitrification process, so as not to overload the capacity of the system to detoxify waste.

One way to keep tabs on the nitrogen "budget" of the aquarium is through measurement of nitrate accumulation. Through appropriate testing and maintenance procedures, one can easily fine-tune the feeding regimen so that the fish get enough without excessive waste. One can also assess the affects of adjustments to the community of organisms. Nitrate monitoring can also facilitate the development of a system that is in biological equilibrium.

Feeding Protocol

To see how nitrate measurement can be used to assess the feeding protocol for a particular aquarium, consider a tank that contains only a single fish. Assume that the aquarium has a functioning biological filter of adequate capacity, and that the initial nitrate concentration has been adjusted to zero. If this fish is fed the same amount of food each day, there will be a constant daily accumulation of nitrate in an amount corresponding to the amount of ammonia released when the food is metabolized. In this example, the daily accumulation may be too small to notice, but repeated testing

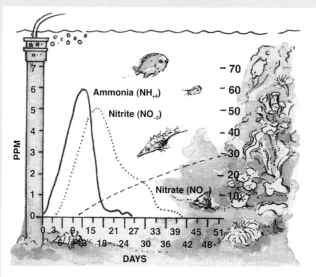

Nitrogen accumulation in the aquarium.

will show a relatively constant rate of increase of nitrate over a longer period of time. If the nitrate level is graphed versus time, a straight line will be obtained. The slope of this line will be different for any given size tank with a given fish community, but will remain constant as long as the fish population is not changed and the feeding rate is constant. Once a base-line graph has been established for a particular tank containing a stable community, the result of a change in feeding schedule will be apparent as a change in the slope of the nitrate accumulation line on the graph.

Checking pH Levels

If the pH of the aquarium is consistently low, first check to see that carbon dioxide is not accumulating. This is done by removing a quart or two of water and aerating it vigorously overnight. Check the pH of both the tank and the aerated water. If the aerated water's pH is 0.2 units or more above that of the tank, carbon dioxide is accumulating. Increased water movement in the aquarium may be all that is needed to alleviate the problem. Keeping the aquarium within a correct range of pH can also be accomplished by the addition of buffering agents designed to increase and stabilize the pH. The use of aragonite sand as part of the substrate can also aid in pH stabilization. As the sand slowly dissolves, ions are released, helping to maintain alkalinity and calcium levels. When the alkalinity of the aquarium is at natural sea-water level or above, the pH tends to remain within a suitably narrow range.

Adding a rounded teaspoon of calcium oxide to a gallon of water produces a saturated solution of limewater.

Adjusting Alkalinity

Alkalinity may be increased by the direct addition of carbonates to the water. This can be accomplished through the use of commercial chemical preparations (such as limewater), or through the dissolution of aragonite sand in the substrate, or by introducing water with a high lime content from a "calcium reactor."

Calcium Concentration

The calcium concentration of the aquarium can be maintained through techniques similar to those for alkalinity maintenance. A simple method that works well is the addition of lime-water to the aquarium. Limewater is prepared by adding dry calcium oxide to distilled water, allowing the mixture to settle, and decanting. The clear supernatant liquid is added to the aquarium to replace all evaporated water. How-ever, because limewater is very alkaline, care must be taken to ensure that additions do not drive the pH above 8.6 for more than a few hours at a time.

GOING FURTHER

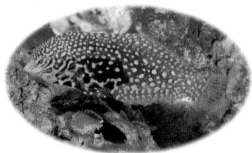

Marine aquarium keeping has come a long way since the first edition of this book. In particular, the Internet has opened up unprecedented opportunities for aquarium enthusiasts to share information.

The Web has become the ultimate reference source for nearly all of us. I have already mentioned FishBase, a compilation of valuable data on roughly 30,000 marine and freshwater species. You can find information about coral reefs in general by searching the vast database at *www.reefbase.org*. Information on invertebrates can be found at *www.species2000.org*. Note that you will need the scientific name of the invertebrate in order to access the Species2000 database.

Researching a topic on the Web can be fun, but sometimes you want the advice of an experienced, like-minded human being. You can connect with thousands by joining an aquarium society. This can be done in person in many large cities, or from anywhere via Internet chat rooms devoted to aquarium keeping. Find a marine aquarium club at the Marine Aquarium Societies of North America site, *www.masna.org*. Plenty of Web sites offer aquarium-keeping advice. Check out *www.reefcentral.com*, for a good example. Beware, though. We all know that anyone can

post anything on the Internet. I suggest confirming relevant information with two to three sources before accepting it as gospel.

I sincerely hope you find your first marine aquarium so rewarding that you will want a second, larger tank. Before you take that step, though, remember that the same operating principles apply to all marine aquariums. Plan first. The value of a carefully researched plan increases when the aquarium represents a big investment. Plenty of options lie out there for you to explore. You can even dive a coral reef in person and bring back specimens for your tank! Just be sure to make all the appropriate arrangements with a travel agency.

Studies have shown that aquarium keeping provides many benefits, including stress relief and a sense of connectedness that our hectic lives often lack. A simple pastime can ultimately inspire a piece of living art adorning your home. Children love aquariums, and find that learning about sea creatures is fun, especially "up close and personal." A beautiful marine aquarium can provide a lifetime of enjoyment for your entire family. I hope this book inspires you to aim for that goal.

A perfectly camouflaged frogfish (**Antennarius maculatus**) *lies in wait for prey.*

GLOSSARY

Alkalinity: The resistance of a solution to a change in pH as acid is added. (Synonyms: carbonate hardness, KH, alkali reserve)

Amphipod: Any of several species of crustaceans, usually smaller than $1/4$ inch (6 mm) in length, distinguished by a laterally compressed body. They are an important component of a healthy aquarium's microfauna.

Amyloodinium: A dinoflagellate fish parasite that often causes death in marine aquarium fish.

Biotope: A community of organisms characteristic of a specific habitat.

Calcification: Extraction of calcium (Ca^{2+}) ions from seawater by any of several types of organisms, including stony corals, echinoderms, and crustaceans.

Copepod: Any of several species of crustaceans, usually just visible to the naked eye, characterized by microscopic anatomical details. They are an important component of a healthy aquarium's microfauna.

Coral reef: A massive underwater structure comprised of the skeletons of living coral polyps, together with associated organisms, including seaweeds, fish, and invertebrates.

Cryptocaryon: A ciliated protozoan parasite of marine fish, often observed in aquarium fish that have been recently subjected to stress.

Element: Substances that cannot be reduced to simpler components by ordinary chemical means.

Flatworm: Any member of the Phylum Platyhelminthes, characterized by a flattened body, simple internal anatomy, and no appendages. They are an important component of a healthy aquarium's microfauna.

Head and lateral line erosion (HLLE): A condition seen in some species of marine fish, thought to arise as a result of dietary deficiency. Loss of pigment and epidermal tissue on the face and head and along the lateral line, is a characteristic symptom.

Ichthyologist: A biologist specializing in fish.

Lateral line: A series of pores, nerve tissue, and canals along both sides of a fish's body that functions in detecting vibrations and water movement, aiding the fish in navigation.

Nutrient: Any organic or inorganic molecule that can be utilized by a living organism for energy production, or as a source of molecular building blocks for growth.

Osmoregulatory: Having to do with maintenance of fluid balance in an organism.

Osmosis: The movement of water molecules across a semi-permeable membrane, such as the membrane surrounding a living cell.

The large eyes and mouth suggest this fish is a nocturnal predator.

Boxfish (Ostracion cubicus) *are toxic; if eaten by a predator, both fish may die.*

pH: The degree of acidity of a solution, expressed as: -log [H$^+$], the negative logarithm of the hydrogen ion concentration in molecules per liter. A pH of 7.0 is neutral, lower values are more acidic, higher values more alkaline.

Photoperiod: The number of hours of sunlight to which an organism is exposed daily.

Protogynous hermaphroditism: A form of sex determination in some fish families, in which all juvenile individuals are female. As individuals mature, they may change into males, depending upon environmental circumstances. The opposite phenomenon, in which individuals start life as males and mature into females, is also known and is called "protandrous hermaphroditism."

Salinity: A measurement of the amount of dissolved solids in a solution, expressed in parts per thousand by weight.

Substrate: The material on the bottom of an aquarium, or any solid object to which an organism is attached or clings to.

Symbiotic: Referring to any of a variety of relationships in which the ecological roles of two species are related in a complex, specific way.

Zooxanthellae: Dinoflagellate algae living in an obligate, mutually beneficial symbiotic relationship with certain species of marine invertebrates.

The blacktail damselfish (Dascyllus melanurus) *remains popular with hobbyists because of its extreme hardiness, despite a tendency to aggressiveness.*

Information about aquariums and aquarium fish can be found in a seemingly endless supply of books, periodicals, and Web sites. Here are a few that might be particularly helpful as you prepare to maintain a marine aquarium.

Books

Borneman, Eric H. (2001) *Aquarium Corals: Selection, Husbandry and Natural History.* Neptune City, NJ: TFH/Microcosm.

This comprehensive reference covers every facet of coral biology and how it relates to their aquarium care, in an accessible, engaging style.

Kurtz, Jeffrey (2002) *The Simple Guide to Marine Aquariums.* Neptune City, NJ: TFH Publications.

A complete, well-illustrated, and environmentally-conscious guide to saltwater aquarium keeping.

Nudibranchs or sea slugs typically sport brilliant coloration, but unfortunately seldom adapt to aquarium life.

Michael, Scott W. (1999) *Marine Fishes: 500 Essential-to-know Aquarium Species.* Shelburne, VT: Microcosm Ltd.

Beautifully illustrated with the author's photographs, this valuable reference includes information on each species' adaptability to aquarium life.

Shimek, Ronald L. (2004) *Marine Invertebrates: 500 Essential-to-know Aquarium Species.* Neptune City, NJ: TFH/Micrososm.

This book covers all the invertebrates you might find in an aquarium dealer's stock, and then some. Lavishly illustrated with color photographs, this book's best feature is an index of Web sites containing information about specific invertebrate groups.

Skomal, Gregory (2002) *Saltwater Aquariums for Dummies.* New York: Hungry Minds, Inc.

Comprehensive coverage of basic techniques, water chemistry, and other topics vital to successful saltwater aquarium management.

Periodicals

Aquarium Fish Magazine
P.O. Box 6050
Mission Viejo, CA 92690-6050
www.aquariumfish.com

Freshwater and Marine Aquarium
P.O. Box 6050
Mission Viejo, CA 92690-6050
www.famamagazine.com/FAMA

Tropical Fish Hobbyist
One TFH Plaza
Neptune City, NJ 07753
www.tfhmagazine.com

The cuttlefish (Sepia sp.) is a fascinating invertebrate predator best suited to a tank by itself.

Internet Sites

www.aquariacentral.com

A gateway site with links to articles, aquarium societies, and much more. Chat online with like-minded hobbyists and get your questions answered by experts.

www.aquarium.net

A mostly commercial site with dozens of links to suppliers of all types of aquarium products.

www.aquariumcouncil.org

The Marine Aquarium Council works to promote sustainable coral reef fisheries through its certification program.

www.aza.org

Founded in 1924, the American Zoo and Aquarium Association (AZA) is a nonprofit organization dedicated to the advancement of zoos and aquariums in the areas of conservation, education, science, and recreation.

www.fishbase.org

Search thousands of listings for individual fish species on this comprehensive Web site. You can search by common or scientific name, family, and a host of other parameters to locate information about all kinds of fish, both common and rare.

www.fishlinkcentral.com

Another portal site with links to dozens of others, including commercial sites, personal homepages, clubs, chat rooms, and much more.

www.marinebio.org/MarineBio

Besides a wealth of information on oceans and conservation, this site features a detailed database of saltwater fish.

www.reefcentral.com

Reef Central is an online community for saltwater aquarium enthusiasts.

INDEX

This edition exclusive in the United States and Canada to:

About the Author

John Tullock's many books on aquarium keeping have sold more than 150,000 copies since 1995. He received a master's degree from the University of Tennessee in 1976, and has worked as a biologist and nature writer ever since. Along the way he owned a retail and mail order aquarium business and operated a wildflower nursery. The American Horticultural Society named his book, *Growing Hardy Orchids* (Timber Press, 2005), one of the five Great Garden Books of 2006. For over 20 years Tullock has served on the board of directors of Conservation Fisheries, a nonprofit organization that has reared thousands of endangered fish for restoration projects and scientific research.

Important Notes

Electrical equipment for aquarium care is described in this book. Please do not fail to read the note below, since otherwise serious accidents could occur.

Water damage from broken glass, overflowing, or tank leaks cannot always be avoided. Therefore you should not fail to take out insurance.

Please take special care that neither children nor adults ever eat any aquarium plants. It can cause substantial health injury. Fish medication should be kept away from children.

Safety Around the Aquarium

Water and electricity can lead to dangerous accidents. Therefore you should make absolutely sure when buying equipment that it is also really suitable for use in an aquarium.
• Every technical device must have the UL sticker on it. These letters give the assurance that the safety of the equipment has been carefully checked by experts and that "with ordinary use" (as the experts say) nothing dangerous can happen.
• Always unplug any electrical equipment before you do any cleaning around or in the aquarium.
• Never do your own repairs on the aquarium or the equipment if there is something wrong with it. As a matter of principle, all repairs should only be carried out by an expert.

Photo Credits

Aaron Norman: pages 2-3, 4, 5, 7, 8, 9, 10, 11, 12, 13, 14, 15, 17, 18, 19 (right), 20, 21, 25 (bottom), 28, 29, 31 (top), 34 (top), 35, 36 (top), 37 (top left), 40 (right), 41 (bottom), 43, 45, 49 (top), 51, 52, 53 (top), 56, 68, 88, 90, 91, 92, 93; Buscis and Somerville: page 30; Mark Smith: pages 6, 16, 19 (left), 25 (top), 26, 27, 31 (bottom), 32, 33, 36 (bottom), 37 (top right and bottom), 38, 39, 40 (left), 41 (top), 49 (bottom), 53 (bottom), 57, 59, 60, 69, 70, 75, 77, 79, 84, 89; Zig Leszczynski: pages 23, 24, 34 (bottom), 42, 61, 63, 76, 78, 85.

Cover Photos

Front, Back, Inside front, and Inside back: Mark Smith.

All inquiries should be addressed to:
Barron's Educational Series, Inc.
250 Wireless Boulevard
Hauppauge, NY 11788
www.barronseduc.com

ISBN-13: 978-0-7641-6164-3
ISBN-10: 0-7641-6164-4

Library of Congress Catalog Card No. 2007029401

Library of Congress Cataloging-in-Publication Data
Tullock, John H., 1951–
    Your first marine aquarium / by John H. Tullock.
        p. cm.
    Includes bibliographical references and index.
    ISBN-13: 978-0-7641-6164-3 (alk. paper)
    ISBN-10: 0-7641-6164-4 (alk. paper)
    1. Marine aquariums. I. Title.

SF457.1.T867 2008
639.34'2—dc22   2007029401

Printed in China
9 8 7 6 5 4 3 2 1